GREAT WALKS
LAKE DISTRICT

GREAT WALKS

LAKE DISTRICT

COLIN SHELBOURN
Photography by David Ward
Series Editor Frank Duerden

PP

To F.W.S

This special edition has been
produced in 1992
by New Orchard Editions Ltd,
Villiers House, 41/47 Strand,
London WC2N 5JE,
a Cassell company
for publication
by Printwise Publications Ltd,
47 Bradshaw Road, Tottington,
Bury, Lancs BL8 3PW

Reprinted 1993

Photography by David Ward

Printed and bound in Spain by Graficromo S.A.

ISBN 1-87222631-0

Half title page *'The Raven' berthed at Glenridding, Ullswater*

Title page *Lake Windermere from the summit of Wansfell*

CONTENTS

ACKNOWLEDGMENTS

I am very grateful to a number of people who have contributed towards the preparation of this book: in particular, John Wyatt and Frank Duerden, for suggesting my name in the first place; Barry Tullet and Peter Rodgers, both of the Lake District National Park Authority, for their painstaking efforts in proofreading the typescript.

In addition, my grateful thanks to friends and colleagues who have been dragged—willingly or otherwise—into my projects: these include my sister, Lorna, for suggestions regarding routes; Pam Williamson, for invaluable advice on gradients; Malcolm Guyatt, for giving me a lift back to Ravenglass after I missed the train by twenty-four hours; Eileen and Elwyn Morgan, for allowing me to plunder their knowledge of the area over the years. And finally, huge thanks to Pam Grant, for photocopying beyond the call of friendship.

INTRODUCTION

Any book which calls itself *Great Walks of the Lake District* is asking for trouble. Inevitably, there will be people who can think of 'greater' walks than the ones I have selected. Where is Aira Force? Where's the Kentmere Horseshoe? Where is the Pillar route (or whatever)? Well, the list had to be limited somehow; there are over 1500 miles (2414 km) of public footpaths in the Lake District National Park. Complete all the walks in this book and you will have covered 174 miles (280 km) of them.

Certain routes were clearly mandatory. I had to include the highest point in England (but from which route?). Similarly, Helvellyn, High Street, Fairfield and Skiddaw—all summits familiar to even the most casual fellwalker. They have been covered before and no doubt other writers will cover them again, but I hope I offer a personal perspective on the old favourites, plus an occasional, less-familiar route amongst the remaining walks.

The walks are graded for difficulty and a range is offered, beginning with very easy routes which are suitable for families in almost any weather, to more severe routes which require a certain amount of preparation and experience. I have also tried to offer some variety in the high-level walks. Some walkers prefer to gain height as quickly as possible, but my preference is to go up slowly. That way I convince myself that it is less hard work. I don't mind coming down quickly; I've usually got a pub or tea shop in view by then. The low-level walks will inevitably be the more crowded during the summer and at weekends, but there are a few—especially those on the west coast—which can match anything the high fells have to offer in terms of solitude and refreshment. Muncaster Fell is a personal favourite of mine.

When I blithely announced to my friends that I was writing a 'walks' book, their response was unanimous: 'Not another book of Lake District walks'! Once they realized that it meant I could go walking on the fells throughout the week and still call it work, they went very quiet.

The summer of 1986 was a good one, for once. Thanks to Ian McCaskill and my trusty barometer, I only got soaked once. The previous year, a similar project had coincided with one of the wettest summers on record. My notes looked as if I had written them underwater. This time, I decided, it would be different and I bought one of those small Sony cassette recorders. So, I swopped the joy of trying to decipher papier-mâché notebooks for the fun of changing batteries in howling winds half-way along Striding Edge. If any of you were walking the fells last summer and encountered a solitary figure striding about, muttering into his jacket, it wasn't some strange, Lakeland apparition, it was probably me, researching this book.

I was not the only one braving the radiation clouds last year; spare a thought too for David Ward, the photographer. I felt almost guilty every time I suggested a new route, knowing that he would have to make a tortuous ascent, carrying very heavy and very expensive camera equipment. The results of his endeavours are a series of superb photographs which capture the beauty and power of the landscape. I am sure they will encourage many others to follow the routes outlined in this book, for there is no finer way than through taking to the track of coming to know and love the Lake District.

THE LAKE DISTRICT NATIONAL PARK

It was William Wordsworth who first gave birth to the idea of the Lake District as a National Park. Writing in the 1835 edition of his *Guide to the Lakes*, he voiced his concern at the impact new landowners were making upon the landscape and expressed the hope that some form of control could be exercised to moderate their activities:

'In this wish the author will be joined by persons of pure taste throughout the whole island, who, by their visits (often repeated) to the Lakes in the North of England, testify that they deem the district a sort of national property, in which every man has a right and interest who has an eye to perceive and a heart to enjoy.'

Wordsworth's ideas did not become a reality in England until 1949 and the passing of the National Parks and Access to the Countryside Act. This defined a national park as: 'An extensive area of beautiful and relatively wild country in which, for the nation's benefit and by appropriate national decision and action, a) the characteristic landscape beauty is strictly preserved, b) access and facilities for public open-air enjoyment are amply provided, c) wild-life and buildings and places of architectural and historic interest are suitably protected, while d) established farming use is effectively maintained.'

The Lake District was the second National Park to be designated, in 1951, but is the largest at 880 sq miles (227,919 hectares). Today there are ten National Parks, in England and Wales, accounting for perhaps one tenth of the total area of these two countries.

Following local government re-organization in 1974, the statutory authority for the Lake District National Park became known as the Lake District Special Planning Board. The chief administrator is the National Park Officer, who is responsible to a board consisting of thirty members appointed by various bodies: Cumbria County Council, the Secretary of State for the Environment and the four District Councils whose areas fall within the Park.

The National Park Authority (NPA) itself can be broken down into four quite distinct areas of activity, each one the responsibility of a separate department. Administration and the Land Use and Planning Department are both based at the Authority's Kendal headquarters. Within the National Park, the

Key to lakes

1. Bassenthwaite Lake
2. Derwent Water
3. Ullswater
4. Loweswater
5. Crummock Water
6. Buttermere
7. Thirlmere
8. Ennerdale Water
9. Haweswater
10. Wast Water
11. Grasmere
12. Rydal Water
13. Elterwater
14. Windermere
15. Esthwaite Water
16. Coniston Water

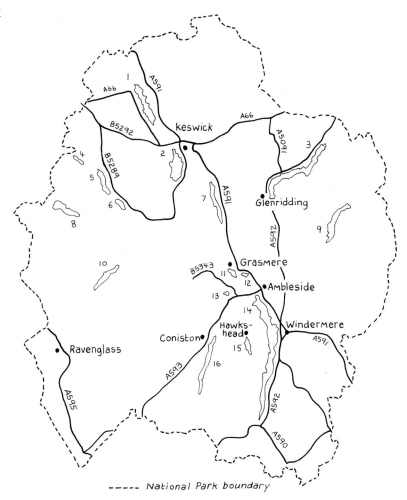

----- National Park boundary

FIGURE 1 The Lake District National Park showing major roads, towns and villages, and lakes

Authority carries out all the planning functions which would otherwise be undertaken by the County Council or the District Councils. Based at the National Park Visitor Centre, Brockhole, are the departments responsible for Park Management and Visitor Services.

What used to be referred to as the Ranger Service now falls under the auspices of Park Management and as such it supplements the department's work in such fields as upland management, maintenance of footpaths and Board properties, liaison with farmers and local landowners. It also works closely with conservation volunteers, through such groups as the British Trust for Conservation Volunteers. The rangers also have an important part to play in educating the public in awareness of fell safety and winter walking requirements. At the time of writing, there are twelve full-time rangers, backed up during the summer by seasonal rangers and around 350 year-round Voluntary Wardens.

Contact with the public results in some blurring of distinction between the duties of the ranger service and those of Visitor Services. This department is responsible for the running of the National Park's nine information centres, together with a number of small information points in local shops. It also runs a caravan park at Silecroft, a boating centre on Coniston Water, a residential centre near Threlkeld and, of course, the National Park Visitor Centre, Brockhole, on the shores of Lake Windermere. This is a large house, standing in its own landscaped grounds, which provides exhibitions, talks, slide shows, courses and displays, all designed to introduce visitors to the area and help them to make the best of their stay here.

A good idea of the full range of services on offer to the visitor can be gleaned from the Lake District Guardian, an annual newspaper published by the National Park which gives details of talks, courses, guided walks and a programme of events throughout the year. It is available, free, from any National Park Information Centre (see Appendix for a list of addresses and telephone numbers).

Great Gable from Brandreth

SOME FACTS AND FIGURES ABOUT THE LAKE DISTRICT NATIONAL PARK

DESIGNATED

13 August 1951. The Park was second of the ten National Parks to be designated, after the Peak District.

AREA

880 sq miles (227,919 hectares) and the largest of the National Parks. Snowdonia is the second largest, with an area of 838 sq miles (217,100 hectares).

EMBLEM

A view of the head of Wastwater, showing Great Gable flanked by Kirk Fell and Lingmell.

POPULATION

The total resident population within the National Park was 40,674 people, according to the 1981 census. Almost 24% were retired and the number of children under fourteen years of age had fallen from 21% in 1971 to 17% in 1981. The population figure in total has hardly changed at all in the last thirty years—in 1951 it was 40,500.

LAND OWNERSHIP

Who owns the National Park? Well, not the NPA, as we've already established—although they do own a tiny segment, around 20,554 acres (8,318 hectares). The largest single landowner by far is the National Trust, with 124,620 acres (50,433 hectares). Next comes the North West Water Authority, with 38,450 acres (15,561 hectares), and the Forestry Commission, with 31,466 (12,734 hectares). In terms of percentages, the figures are:

National Trust	21.7%
North West Water Authority	6.9%
Forestry Commission	5.7%
NPA	3.9%
Ministry of Defence	0.2%

But of the total area of the Park, over 61% is still in private hands.

NATIONAL PARK STATISTICS

Total area of National Park	554,245 acres (224,303 hectares)
Area covered by lakes and reservoirs	16,062 acres (6,500 hectares)
Area under crops	9,227 acres (3,734 hectares)
Area under grass	188,446 acres (76,264 hectares)
Area of rough grazing	153,652 acres (62,128 hectares)
Area of common land	151,225 acres (61,201 hectares)
Area of broadleaved woodland	25,698 acres (10,400 hectares)
Total area of woodland	60,540 acres (24,501 hectares)

THE FACE OF THE LAKE DISTRICT

DRYSTONE WALLS

Conduct a straw poll amongst the visitors leaving the National Park, asking them what impressed them most about the area, and there is a fair chance that a substantial percentage will reply, 'the stone walls'.

Drystone walls—that is, walls built without the aid of cement or mortar—are not unique to the Lake District, but they are an integral part of the landscape. They pattern the valleys, etch the fellsides, and travel in apparently ruler-straight lines for miles at a time. The walls have been part of Lakeland for many hundreds of years; there is a low turf and stone dyke in Eskdale which was built by the Cistercian monks of Furness Abbey during the closing decades of the thirteenth century. By the time of the dissolution of the monasteries, in the sixteenth century, there were walls enclosing drained or cleared land in many settlements throughout the area. Many of these enclosures can be seen today, identifiable by their more rounded corners.

A small fern thrives in a drystone wall

Most of the Lake District stone walls were built following the General Enclosure Act of 1801, which enforced rights over the common land. By the mid-nineteenth century, the greater part of the pattern of walls in the Lake District had been established.

Stone walls do not only serve as field boundaries; many provide shelter for sheep; some have been built to prevent stock from straying into gullies or falling down crags. Others take the form of funnels, open to fellside, and narrowing to culminate in a sheep fold, to assist with the gathering of sheep. Some have acted simply as stone dumps, to clear a valley floor of rock and boulders (a good example is Wasdale Head, where the walls are massive and numerous).

Building a drystone wall is a highly skilled job (those keen to learn can try their hand at the National Park Visitor Centre or go for a day's drystone walling with a ranger). They are built on a foundation of two parallel rows of large, square boulders, lain either side of a three- or four-foot wide trench. The sides or 'faces' of the wall are built up, the inside being filled with smaller stones and rubble, known as 'hearting'. At intervals the two faces are linked by 'through stones', to give the wall strength and prevent it from 'bellying-out'. As the height increases, the stones are set in slightly so that the wall is wider at the base than the top, which vastly increases stability. The top is set with 'cam-stones'—slates placed on edge to discourage sheep from climbing over the wall (alas, this only works on the four-legged variety).

Occasionally, you will come across regular holes in the walls, at ground level. The larger of these are called 'hogg-holes', designed to allow young lambs to pass between fields. Less common are much smaller apertures, known as 'smoots', which are placed in the wall at strategic points to facilitate the catching of rabbits.

It is recorded that in 1877 it would have cost around six shillings and sixpence to build seven yards of drystone wall. A century later that price had increased to £233. Bear this in mind the next time you are tempted to take a short cut.

GEOLOGY OF THE LAKE DISTRICT

The hills of Lakeland are amongst the oldest in the world; Skiddaw, for example, is more ancient than the Alps or the Himalayas. The youngest rocks found anywhere in the Lake District are more than 200 million years old. The geology of the region falls into a distinct pattern.

Around the boundary of the National Park there is an

outcrop of limestone which gives rise to rich plant-life and scenery, quite distinct from any amongst the central fells. Beyond this, working outwards, is an outer ring of red sandstone, such as can be seen at St Bees Head. In the middle of these two rings is the Lake District, which itself can be split into three quite distinct geological regions.

The oldest rocks are those which stretch from Grasmoor to Skiddaw and Blencathra. Known as the Skiddaw Slates, these were laid down by a sedimentary process during the Ordovician period, around 450 million years ago. Hardened and compressed on the beds of shallow seas, much of it has become slate. It is a resistant material which splits along distinct planes and results in a mountain scenery that has steep, smooth, regular ridges.

Along a line from Maiden Moor to Fleetwith Pike, there is a band of rock known as the Borrowdale Volcanic Series. It was formed during a period of intense volcanic activity when ash and lava were laid down into large, jagged boulders of varying textures. Further complexities were introduced by the shattering and cracking produced in various strata by earth movement associated with this volcanic activity. The result is the more rough, angular landscape of the central fells.

A thin band of limestone, known as the Coniston Limestone, separates the Borrowdale Volcanic Series from the softer rocks of the south.

The Borrowdale Volcanics are overlaid by a band that covers the south of the National Park, across Coniston Water to Windermere and beyond to Kendal. Produced by sedimentary action, this is known as the Silurian series. These rocks give rise to softer landscape of smaller hills and gentle slopes and the various rocks which make up this area are reflected in many of the walls and local buildings.

The Ice Age was the final sculptor of the landscape we see today. Geologically speaking, this was a comparatively recent occurrence. Around one million years ago the climate deteriorated so that the heavy snowfalls of winter became extended throughout summer. The snow accumulated, compacted, became ice and flowed south in an enormous sheet which reached the Midlands, before retreating with the rising temperature. Only the highest peaks of Lakeland protruded above the ice. This happened four times, the last retreat occurring only 8,000 years ago—barely yesterday, in geological time. It is still uncertain whether this pattern of freeze and thaw has ended, or whether we are merely enjoying a brief warm spell between ice ages.

The advance of the glaciers gouged straight, narrow dales. The corries (also called combes) formed on northern- and eastern-facing slopes where accumulations of ice flowed down to meet the valley glaciers. Ridges between two or more corries were reduced to narrow aretes—such as Sharp Edge on Blencathra and Striding Edge on Helvellyn.

The rock quarried by the glacier was carried along in the ice, to be dumped as the ice retreated, forming irregular mounds (moraines), especially obvious today at valley heads. Scratched or striated rock slabs show the direction of ice flow. Many of the region's most spectacular waterfalls are the result of tributary valleys left hanging high up the sides of ice-deepened dales.

Once the ice had finally retreated, rocks were laid bare and the mountain slopes were free to be colonized by plants.

MAN AND THE LANDSCAPE

Despite the impression of permanency and wildness, man has influenced and changed the landscape of the Lake District over many centuries. The dominance or decline of various social and economic factors have led to a constantly changing pattern of land use.

The first settlers started the process by beginning to clear the forests which had colonized all but the highest fell tops after the Ice Age. Stone axes locally produced from a special type of rock were efficient tools. Examples of the local implements have been found even in the south of England, showing a high degree of entrepreneurial skill for men usually thought of as 'primitive'. The later development of bronze and iron tools speeded the clearing of tree cover. By Roman times much of the primitive woodland had been cleared, with the exception of inaccessible sites. The Romans left some superb examples of their engineering ability—Hardknott Fort and the several Roman roads over some of the higher passes testify to their influence.

The Norse raiders left the legacy of place names, their monuments being few and mainly at lower levels. The Scandinavians are also credited with the introduction of sheep to the area (although there is also some suggestion that the local Herdwicks are the descendants of stock washed ashore from the ill-fated Spanish Armada). What is not in doubt is that the Herdwick, an extremely hardy beast, is ideally suited to the mountainous terrain.

A flock of the grey-coated, white-faced, sturdy animals have a strong homing instinct, dispensing with the need to fence large

A dramatic view of Blea Water from above Long Stile, a classic example of a glaciated corrie

areas of open fell. In addition, they can survive on the fell in the roughest weather. Occasionally, in a particularly harsh winter, Herdwicks have been dug out of a snowdrift up to a month after they were first buried! Less to its credit is its habit of grazing on young saplings, and stripping bark from tree trunks when grazing is poor. The grassy uplands of the high fell land are kept clear of tree cover by the sheep's voracious habit.

Despite the Herdwick's attachment to its native fell, Medieval man enclosed vast tracts of the low-lying valleys. Wool trading was the basis of wealth for the Cistercian monasteries, and cereal crops were also raised, leading to a network of granaries or 'granges' to store the produce. Routes were deftly engineered to allow strings of packhorses to travel to the markets.

Later, the use of water power led to the development of supporting industries. Spinning, carding, weaving and fulling were all activities based on water power. Kendal has even given its name to a particular coarse woollen cloth, the Kendal Green, famous in Shakespeare's day. The town motto is still 'wool is my bread'. The cloth industry declined in the early nineteenth century when material from Spain became popular.

Today traditional hill farming is still under pressure from modern developments. It would be fitting to protect and encourage traditional methods which are so suitable for an upland area, and have played such a large part in the formation of the landscape.

MINING IN THE LAKE DISTRICT

A wealth of geologically different types of rock often gives rise to a wide range of mineral ores. The Romans were the first to notice the rich pickings. But it was not until the sixteenth and seventeenth centuries that mining in the Lake District actively increased.

In 1564, the Company of the Mines Royal was empowered to 'search, dig, try, roast and melt all manner of mines and ores of gold, silver, copper and quick-silver'. The Crown took 10% of all gold and silver—and the lion's share of 'all Pretious stones or pearl to be found'.

Keswick became a boom town as a result. In 1565 some forty or so German miners came to the Lake District (even today several local families have surnames of Germanic origin for the early miners stayed long enough to court and marry local girls). By 1567, Keswick had become a thriving town with six furnaces in operation. Why German miners? Simply that their skills represented the height of technical achievement in the Elizabethan period.

The ore came from the Borrowdale Volcanic rocks and the Skiddaw slates. The mines were pumped dry using an ingenious system of rag 'sponges' which were lowered into the shafts with the aid of water power. The use of water as a power source necessitated the channelling and damming of fell streams. With the aid of their technology, amazing depths were reached. Even so, the mines must have been damp and dangerous, and the work hard.

Woodland industries, especially the production of charcoal, also became important. Ore needed to be smelted in bloomeries. Nor were the woodlands merely exploited, since the importance of conservation management was understood. Basket-makers, tanners, wood-turning, swill-making (a swill was a kind of basket) and other cottage industries bloomed as the wealth of the region increased.

By the late eighteenth century, the Lake District had become an important producer of roofing slate. Whereas the Caldbeck Fells, Newlands Valley, Glenridding, Keswick and Coniston areas were important for mining, Tilberthwaite, Honister, Coniston and Langdale were slate-quarrying centres. Increasing urban development brought an ever-increasing demand for the slates until production reached a peak in the 1890s.

Skills were handed down from father to son, ensuring a strong family tradition. The durability of many of the smaller buildings testify to the knowledge the local folk brought to their work. Indeed some of the villages and hamlets would not have been built if it had not been for the industry of the region.

Truly the Lake District can be said to be an ex-industrial landscape, for the mining and quarrying of its natural wealth have shaped the landscape.

NATIONAL TRUST

The National Park Authority (as it prefers to be known) should not be confused with the National Trust. Both were formed to care for and conserve the countryside; both promote the area with information centres throughout the Lake District; both have rangers (although the NT calls them wardens, as did the NPA originally). The NPA, however, is a statutory body, receiving the bulk of its funding from government and local councils; the National Trust is a registered charity which depends for its income upon revenue generated by its properties and upon the continued goodwill of its members and supporters.

The NPA does not own the Lake District—unlike national parks in the USA—whereas the National Trust owns, or leases or holds covenants over all the land and buildings it protects. In many ways, this makes the NT's responsibility greater, though, conversely, it also renders it less accountable to the local community. The National Trust owns almost a quarter of the land within the National Park boundary, including a large part of the central fells of Lakeland.

The National Trust for Places of Historic Interest or Natural Beauty, to give it its full title, was officially registered on 12 January 1895. It has many of its roots in the Lake District; Canon Hardwicke Rawnsley, Vicar of Crosthwaite (near Keswick), Victorian all-rounder and vigorous campaigner in countryside matters was one of the three founders of the Trust. The first property purchased by the Trust was Brandelhow Woods, on the shores of Derwent Water, acquired in 1902.

Today, the Trust's most famous properties in the Lake District are Beatrix Potter's house, in Near Sawrey, and Tarn

Seathwaite Farm, Borrowdale

Hows, near Hawkshead. The Trust's regional headquarters are in Ambleside and they have information shops in Grasmere, Keswick, Hawkshead, Ambleside and Cockermouth.

Tourism and the Lake District

One of the earliest guide books to the Lake District was published in 1778, and written by Thomas West, a Scottish Jesuit priest, born around 1720. Entitled *A Guide to the Lakes, in Cumberland, Westmorland, and Lancashire* it was the first guide to treat the area in terms of picturesque mountain scenery (previous writers had considered the region to be a wild, desolate sort of place, where one would encounter nothing but discomfort and inconvenience). The book was a best seller. After West's death in 1779, the Guide was enlarged with additional engravings and the text heavily expanded. It taught a generation of travellers to regard the scenery of Lakeland as if it were a painting—preferably by one of the great landscape artists, such as Claude, Salvator or Poussin—and was the most popular book on the Lakes for almost half a century.

In 1810, a reverend gentleman by the name of Joseph Wilkinson issued a collection of sketches and drawings. Accompanying his work was an anonymous essay about the Lake District. Its author was William Wordsworth. Wordsworth was clearly none too enamoured of Wilkinson's skills as he rewrote the essay and re-issued it—shorn of the drawings—in 1822. The definitive edition was released in 1835, and became known simply as *A Guide to the Lakes*. It became an even greater success than West's Guide; so much so that at the height of Wordsworth's fame as a poet, he is reputed to have been approached and asked whether he had written anything else, in addition to his Guide!

The arrival of the railways marked the real beginning of the tourist age. The line from London to Carlisle was opened in 1846. A branch line was proposed to run into southern Lakeland and—despite vociferous protestations from Wordsworth—was opened in 1847. It ended at the tiny hamlet of Birthwaite, which blossomed almost overnight into the village we now know as Windermere. The Furness railway was opened to Coniston in 1859, and in 1865 a line connected Cockermouth, Keswick and Penrith. There were even plans afoot for a scenic railway to the summit of Skiddaw.

Passengers were able to catch steam launches on Lake Windermere from 1845 and in 1859 the original Gondola set sail on Coniston Water.

Tourism is now one of the largest employers in the Lake District; over 25,000 people are either directly or indirectly involved—or around 13% of the total workforce. In addition to the National Park, the area is promoted by the Cumbria Tourist Board, most of the District Councils, various trading organizations and a number of town and village publicity associations. Around ten million people visit the National Park on day trips, plus another three million staying overnight, each year. Nowadays, 90% of all visitors to the Park come by private car; 14.5 million people live within three hours drive of the Lake District—a sobering thought. One August Sunday in 1974, 60,000 vehicles entered the National Park, adding 180,000 people to the 50,000 or so already on holiday in the area.

What do visitors do here? A survey of people on holiday revealed the following: 34% were picnicking; 32% admiring the view; 28% were walking. Only 10% of the total number of people interviewed were fellwalkers. So even today, when the need to care for the area is greater than ever before due to the pressure of visitors, it should still be possible to find peace and solitude on the fells.

SELECTED WALKS IN THE LAKE DISTRICT NATIONAL PARK

INTRODUCTION TO THE ROUTE DESCRIPTIONS

1. ACCESS (see page 186)

The majority of walks are along paths for which there is public right-of-way. One or two routes have been included to which this does not apply, but which have, as far as is known, been walked for a long time without objection and it is not expected therefore that difficulties will be encountered. 'Short cuts' that might lead to proliferation of paths or to the annoyance of local people should not be taken. Paths are sometimes diverted officially by the National Park Authority, for example to allow a badly-eroded path to recover. The diversion will usually be well-marked. In such cases, of course, the diversion should always be followed.

2. ASCENT

The amount of climbing involved in each route has been estimated from Outdoor Leisure or 1:50 000 maps as appropriate and should be regarded as approximate only.

3. CAR-PARKS

The nearest public car-park is given. There will be many places where a car can be parked by the wayside, but it must be done with care, as indiscriminate parking can be a great nuisance to local people.

4. INTERESTING FEATURES ON THE ROUTE

The best position for seeing these is indicated both in the route descriptions and on the maps by *(1), (2),* etc.

5. LENGTH

These are strictly 'map miles' estimated from the Outdoor Leisure or 1:50 000 maps; no attempt has been made to take into account any ascent or descent involved.

Previous page *Helm Crag from Grasmere*

FIGURE 2 Location of routes, as shown on OS Outdoor Leisure maps (NB the four sheets overlap to some extent)

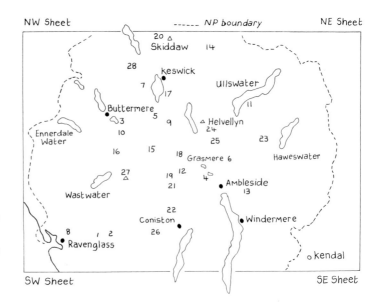

6. MAPS The maps are drawn to a scale of approximately 1:25 000 (see page 26) and all names are as given on the Outdoor Leisure maps. Field boundaries in particular, which can be a mixture of hedge, fence and wall, should be taken as a 'best description'. The maps have been drawn in the main, so that the route goes from the bottom to the top of a page. This will enable the reader to 'line up' the map in the direction walked whilst still holding the book in the normal reading position. The arrow on each map points to grid north. The scale of some small features has been slightly exaggerated for clarity. For easy cross-reference, the relevant Outdoor Leisure sheets are indicated on each map.

7. ROUTE DESCRIPTION The letters 'L' and 'R' stand for left and right respectively. Where these are used for changes of direction then they imply a turn of about 90° when facing in the direction of the walk. 'Half L' and 'half R' indicate a half-turn, i.e. approximately 45°, and 'back half L' or 'back half R' indicate three quarter-turns, i.e. about 135°. PFS stands for 'Public Footpath Sign', PBS for 'Public Bridleway Sign' and OS for 'Ordnance Survey'.

To avoid constant repetition, it should be assumed that all stiles and gates mentioned in the route description are to be crossed (unless there is a specific statement otherwise).

8. STANDARD OF THE ROUTES The briefest examination of the route descriptions that follow will show that the routes described cover an enormous range of both length and of difficulty; the easiest can probably be undertaken by a family party at almost any time of the year whilst the hardest are only really suitable for experienced fellwalkers who are both fit and well-equipped. Any walker therefore who is contemplating following a route should make sure before starting that it is within his or her ability.

It is not easy in practice however to give an accurate picture of the difficulty of any route, because it is dependent upon a number of factors and will in any case vary considerably from day to day with the weather. Any consideration of weather conditions must, of course, be left to the walker himself (but read the section on safety first). Apart from that, it is probably best to attempt an overall assessment of difficulty based upon the length, amount of ascent and descent, problems of route-finding and finally, upon the roughness of the terrain.

Each of the routes has therefore been given a grading based upon a consideration of these factors and represented by the bold numerals which precedes each walk title. A general description of each grade follows:

Easy (1) Generally short walks (up to 5 miles, 8 km) over well-defined paths, with no problems of route-finding. Some climbing may be involved, but mostly over fairly gradual slopes with only short sections of more difficult ground.

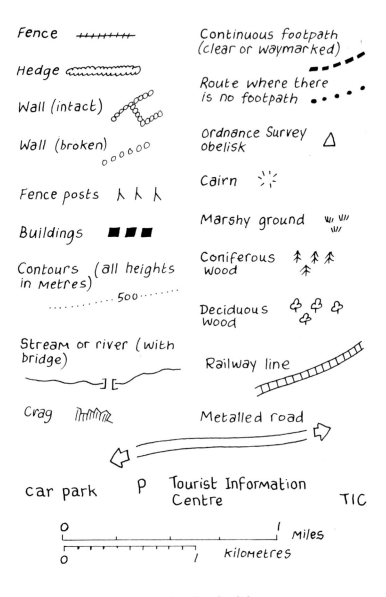

Fence

Hedge

Wall (intact)

Wall (broken)

Fence posts

Buildings

Contours (all heights in metres)

Stream or river (with bridge)

Crag

car park   P

Continuous footpath (clear or waymarked)

Route where there is no footpath

Ordnance Survey obelisk

Cairn

Marshy ground

Coniferous wood

Deciduous wood

Railway line

Metalled road

Tourist Information Centre   TIC

Miles

kilometres

FIGURE 3 Symbols used on detailed route maps

Moderate (2) Rather longer walks (up to about 10 miles, 16 km), mostly over paths, but with sections where route-finding will be more difficult. Mountain summits may be reached with climbing over steeper and rougher ground.

More strenuous (3) Perhaps longer walks (10–20 miles, 16–32 km) with prolonged spells of climbing. Some rough ground, calling for good route-finding ability, perhaps with stretches of scrambling.

The walks are arranged in order of increasing difficulty, so that Route 1 is the easiest and Route 28 the hardest.

9. STARTING AND FINISHING POINTS

A summary of each walk is given at the head of each section with information on length, amount of climbing and any special difficulties, such as scrambling, that will be met along the way. Most of the routes are circular, returning to their starting point, as this avoids any problems with transport when the walk is completed. In the case of the exceptions a local train or lake launch is used to connect the starting and finishing points. The location of each starting point is given by the number of the appropriate Outdoor Leisure (1:25 000) map with a six figure grid reference (see page 188); thus (SE-235123) indicates grid reference 235123 which can be found on the south-east Outdoor Leisure sheet.

10. TIME FOR COMPLETION

The usual method of estimating the length of time needed for a walk is by Naismith's Rule; 'For ordinary walking allow one hour for every 3 miles (5 km) and add one hour for every 2000 feet (600 m) of ascent; for backpacking with a heavy load allow one hour for every 2½ miles (4 km) and one hour for every 1500 feet (450 m) of ascent'. However, for many this tends to be over-optimistic and it is better for each walker to form an assessment of his own performance over one or two walks. Naismith's Rule also makes no allowance for rest or food stops or for the influence of weather conditions.

Stanley Force

STARTING AND FINISHING
POINT
National Park Authority car park in
the narrow lane opposite the Eskdale
Centre (SW-172004).
LENGTH
2 miles (13.2 km)
ASCENT
330 ft (100 m)

Stanley Force, or Dalegarth Force as it is sometimes known, is widely regarded as Lakeland's loveliest waterfall. A 60 ft (18 m) cascade set in a magnificent ravine, it was acquired under Access Agreements by the NPA in 1964 because of the richness and variety of the surrounding rock formations and plant life. The Force is named after the Stanley family, who live at the nearby Dalegarth Hall.

Route Description (Map 1)

Leave the car park and turn L along the narrow lane. After 150 yards (137 m), you pass a gateway on your R, the entrance to Dalegarth Hall. The lane—now little more than a track—bears L at the gateway (PFS 'Stanley Ghyll and Birker Moor').

You soon come to an iron farm gate across the track and, once through, you begin to bear L, alongside a drystone wall. You pass a pair of fields, one on either side of you; ignore the footpaths off to R and L and carry straight on. After a further 100 yards (91 m), the track bears to the R and directly in front of you is a wooden gate and a National Park Access Area sign: Stanley Ghyll.

Go through the gate and bear R, following a rough footpath to the banks of Stanley Ghyll. Turn R and follow the path upstream. You are walking through very pleasant mixed woodland. The path is loose and rough in places and becomes indistinct at times. Cross over a small wooden footbridge, which takes you across the course of a dried up river bed, and continue gently uphill. A beck comes in from your R, crossed by stone slabs.

The footpath winds around the contour of the hill on your R and gradually you find yourself entering a deep gorge, lined with oak and rhododendrons. This is a lush, attractive place and the river on your L starts to fall down a series of short cascades.

Stanley Ghyll—one of the precarious-looking bridges on the approach to the waterfalls

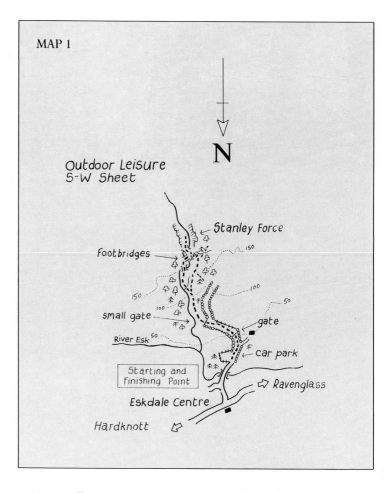

MAP 1

N

Outdoor Leisure
S-W Sheet

Stanley Force

Footbridges

150

150

100

100

50

small gate

gate

River Esk   50

car park

Starting and
Finishing Point

Ravenglass

Eskdale Centre

Hardknott

Eventually, you come to the first of the footbridges, crossing Stanley Ghyll. It looks old and is rather narrow, but it is quite safe. Cross to the other bank and continue uphill.

You climb to a second footbridge and cross again. The footpath climbs away from the bridge for a few yards to encounter a track coming in from your R. Turn L and follow the track to the third and final bridge. As you walk across, you have to step over a small stile bearing a sign which reads: 'Warning— beyond here path unsafe'. As long as you are not wearing high heels, you will be all right for a little while yet. As you come off the bridge and turn R, climbing around a large Scots pine, the path becomes bouldery and muddy and can be very slippery in wet weather. After 10 yards (9 m) you realize that you are quite high above the level of the ghyll. Continue for a few more yards, to round the cliff on your L, and suddenly you are confronted by Stanley Force, in all its glory.

Beyond this point there is a wooden fence blocking the path and a notice indicating that there is no further safe path. This can be frustrating, but it is better to follow the advice. Turn round and reluctantly retrace your steps across the last bridge.

Follow the track back to the point at which the path descends to the second bridge. Go straight on, across a small beck via a series of wooden slats, and bear L following the beck up into the trees.

After 50 yards (45 m), you arrive at a junction in the path, with a small slate footbridge on your L. Go R and the path doubles back on itself to climb uphill through the trees. This path takes you out onto the top of the gorge, though still surrounded by trees and bushes. You can hear the rush of the water away to your R as the path levels out and starts to descend.

The path drops through the trees, passing a smaller path which bears off across the fields to your L. If you go L, you cross a field a via a permissive path which brings you through a farm gate and back onto the original rough lane from the car park. If you continue straight ahead, the path brings you back to Stanley Ghyll and your outgoing route; from there turn L and retrace your steps to the car park.

Stanley Force

THE RIVER ESK

STARTING AND FINISHING
POINT
Dalegarth terminus of the Ravenglass
and Eskdale Railway (SW-174007).
LENGTH
$3\frac{1}{2}$ miles (5.6 km)
ASCENT
83 ft (25 m)

Eskdale is one of the most delightful of the Lake District valleys. It is also one of the most varied; its head lies among the highest mountains in England, its foot at the sea, at Ravenglass. This walk follows a short section of the River Esk as it coils and loops along the valley floor.

ROUTE DESCRIPTION (Map 2)

From the station car park turn L and follow the road as far as the crossroads at Brook House. Turn R, along a cart-track (signed: St Catherine's Church). To your L, as you follow the track between the stone walls, there is an impressive view of Hardknott and Scafell Pike. Continue along the track until you pass a small group of houses on your L, whereupon the track bears R slightly (PFS 'church and river'). You walk past Esk View Farm and through two farm gates across the track to reach St Catherine's Church *(1)*.

The track peters out on the riverbank, just beyond the church. Turn L (PFS 'Doctor Bridge') and follow the Esk upstream. After 150 yards (136 m) you will pass through a farm gate and the path splits three ways. Bear R, and follow the wall towards the river. At a gap in the wall, cross through to discover a delightful, tree-lined gorge and the remains of an old railway bridge. From the gorge, cross back over the wall and follow the wall on your R uphill to a gateway. Go through and straight ahead, between two stone walls. Hartley Crag is the imposing rock face on your R. The path climbs quite high above the river and you will cross a small beck which floods the path. Continue to a kissing gate. Go through and follow the path for another 400 yards (364 m) until you come to a pair of farm gates in a stone wall in front of you. Go through the R-hand gate.

You now start to get brilliant views of the fells ahead of you and, on your R, Birker Force cascades through a dramatic cleft in Gate Crag. Disregard a gap in the stone wall on your L and follow the path to descend back to the riverbank. The far bank is lined with trees and you should look out for an attractive little

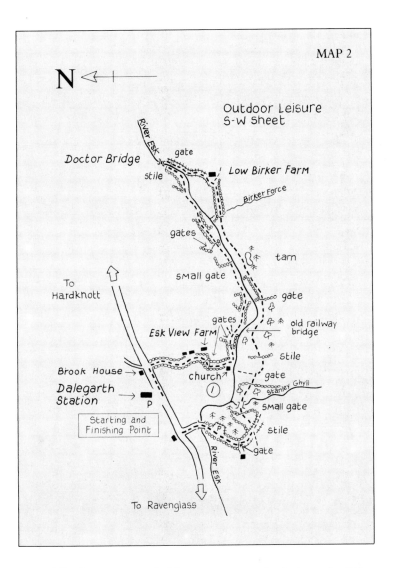

MAP 2

Outdoor Leisure S-W sheet

'Tommy' Dobson's headstone, St Catherine's Church

waterfall, almost concealed by rowan as it feeds into the Esk.

After you have been following the river for just over a mile (1.6 km), you cross a stile and find yourself on a minor road alongside Doctor Bridge. Turn R and cross over the picturesque bridge and then turn R again (PBS 'Dalegarth') and through a farm gate (disregarding the stile in the fence on your L). Follow the track as it bears uphill to Low Birker Farm. As you pass the farm buildings, the track bears R slightly, between two stone walls.

Shortly after passing the farm, you cross a footbridge, directly below Birker Force and then go through a farm gate and straight across a field. You have a good view across the patterns of fields to Dalegarth station. The track continues past a conifer plantation on your L, skirting around a small boggy tarn. As you approach a stone wall, bear L slightly—do not go through the gateway and into the enclosure—and the track winds down to a farm gate in a stone wall ahead of you. Go through and into the woods. The path is rocky and can be flooded along here after heavy rainfall.

Leave the woods via a stile and follow the track across the fields for another 500 yards (455 m) until you come to a fork. Only the R-hand path is signposted (PFS 'St Catherine's Church, Boot'). Go L, to cross a small beck and follow the track across open heath towards a large, older-looking wood. You come to a stone wall; go through the farm gate and descend through the trees to a long, narrow footbridge, crossing Stanley Ghyll.

Go straight across the footbridge and up to a small gate in a stone wall. This brings you into a field, often used as a campsite during the summer. Go straight across the field to a fence opposite and cross via a stile. You are now standing on a rough track, with another field in front of you (signed: 'bridleway to Forge Bridge'). Do not cross the track to the next field, instead turn R and follow the track downhill.

After 100 yards (91 m) you will come to a farm gate. Go through and continue along the cart-track, with conifer woods on either side. The track takes you past the car park which was the start for the Stanley Ghyll walk. Follow the track until you reach the main road, then turn R and follow the road 300 yards (273 m) back to Dalegarth Station.

1 St Catherine's Church

A plain, unimposing building, built of local granite during the seventeenth century. Of particular note is the churchyard, which contains a memorial to 'Tommy' Dobson, once master of the Eskdale and Ennerdale foxhounds. His reputation during his lifetime exceeded that of even the great John Peel and on his death, in 1910, the monument was erected by 'nearly 300 friends from all parts of the country'. The stone bears a likeness of Tommy, flanked by a fox and a hound.

Doctor Bridge on the River Esk

1.3

BUTTERMERE

STARTING AND FINISHING
POINT
Buttermere Village. NPA car park
beside the Fish Hotel (NW-175169).
LENGTH
4 miles (6.4 km)
ASCENT
50 ft (15 m)

The quintessence of natural beauty—or so thought the tourists of the nineteenth century. Many today still regard Buttermere—'the lake by the dairy pastures'—as the prettiest of the smaller lakes. A footpath circuits the shore, making it an easy and delightful family walking area. Large sections of this walk are well sheltered—either by trees or, at one point, a rock tunnel!—making it a good route for those days when poor weather renders the high fells inaccessible.

ROUTE DESCRIPTION (Map 3)

Walk back to the car park entrance and bear R, around the front of the Fish Hotel (*1*), to a track (PBS 'Buttermere Lake, Scale Bridge'). Turn R and follow the track for 200 yards (182 m) until you arrive at a farm gate and a fork in the track. Keep L, through a kissing gate and between the fields. Directly in front of you is a waterfall, tumbling down from Bleaberry Tarn; this is Sourmilk Gill (a popular name for Lake District waterfalls—you will encounter two more Sourmilk Gill's during the course of routes elsewhere in this book).

Arriving at another farm gate, cross the stile alongside and continue across the fields to a footbridge. Cross the beck and the path forks again; bear L, along the lake shore towards the trees. As you enter the wood, there is a path on your R, signed Scale Force. Keep L, across a second footbridge and through a kissing gate, into Burtness Wood. After a few yards you will pass another path going up through the trees on your R, to Red Pike. Ignore it and carry straight on, walking along a level, well-made bridle track. This is a lovely path through the woods, walking R along the shore line, with views across the lake to Goat Crag.

After $\frac{1}{2}$ mile (0.8 km), the track appears to split three ways; take the narrower, L-hand path, across a footbridge (a pair of railway sleepers) and continue along the shore. You come to a superb view of Fleetwith Pike. The path meanders along the shore for another 400 yards (364 m) and brings you to a stone

Sheep at Gatesgarth Farm

wall and a kissing gate. Once through, you leave the woods behind and have open fellside on your R, covered with bracken. As you approach the head of the lake, you are joined on your L by a drystone wall. Follow this until you pass a sheep enclosure and arrive at a junction. The path to your R climbs up to Scarth Gap and Haystacks. Go L, though a kissing gate and across a footbridge to follow the track across the fields to Gatesgarth Farm. The track bears L to Gatesgarth Beck and then through a narrow gate, to skirt round to the L of the farmyard and bring you out onto the Honister Pass road.

Turn L and follow the road for 500 yards (455 m) until you return to the lake shore and a narrow, permissive path off to your L. Follow the path to a kissing gate and continue along the shore, through two fields. As you draw closer to a wood, the shore becomes littered with pebbles and it becomes difficult to resist the temptation to try skimming the odd stone across the surface of the lake.

Go through a kissing gate into the woods and you are on a rough footpath which climbs the bank, above the level of the water. Suddenly you find yourself confronted by a tunnel, blasted through the rocks in front of you *(2)*.

Follow the path through the tunnel for 40 yards (36 m) (be warned—the roof is low in places) and you emerge back into daylight on a more level, easily negotiated path. The footpath is now well-defined and straightforward to follow. It leads you through the woods and back out onto fields. You re-enter another small wood. After a quarter-of-a-mile, you come to a

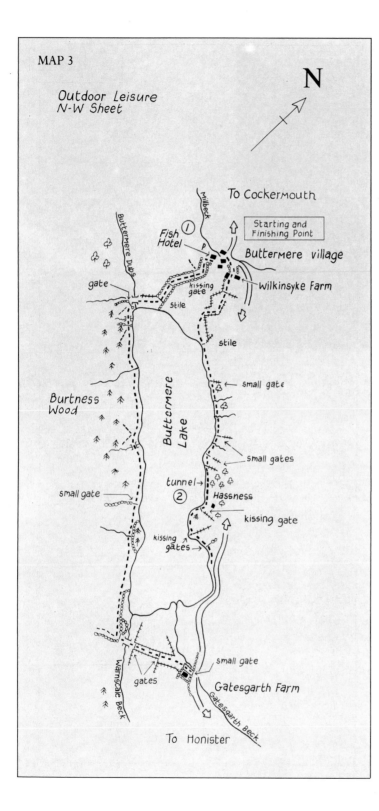

MAP 3

Outdoor Leisure
N-W Sheet

N

To Cockermouth

Starting and
Finishing Point

Fish
Hotel

Buttermere village

Buttermere Dubs

Milbeck

①

P

Wilkinsyke Farm

gate

kissing
gate

stile

stile

small gate

Burtness
Wood

Buttermere Lake

small gates

small gate

tunnel→
②

Hassness

kissing gate

kissing
gates

small gate

Warnscale Beck

gates

Gatesgarth Farm

Gatesgarth Beck

To Honister

View of High Crag, High Stile and Red Pike from Lower Gatesgarth

wire fence and a stile. Cross over and follow the path through another field until you arrive at a small gate. Go through and bear R along a track. This brings you to Wilkinsyke Farm. Go through the farmyard and out onto the main road. Turn L and follow the road back into Buttermere village.

1 The Fish Hotel

Originally The Fish Inn, this was a scene of some excitement in the early years of the nineteenth century when it became the centre of an outrageous scandal. It was the home of Mary Robinson, whose father owned the Inn. A renowned local beauty, her charms were praised by the eccentric writer and traveller, Joseph Budworth, in his *A Fortnight's Ramble in the Lakes*, published in 1792.

Ten years later, the Inn was visited by a gentleman calling himself the Honourable Colonel Alexander Augustus Hope, MP, who came in search of char fishing but caught Mary instead. After a whirlwind romance, during which everyone applauded Mary's good fortune, he married her. The affair was reported in the London *Morning Post*, by their correspondent, Samuel Taylor Coleridge. Once his article appeared, the fun started: Hope's brother, Charles, Earl of Hopetown, expressed grave doubts about the authenticity of the groom as his brother was at that time travelling in Europe. An outcry followed and upon his return from their honeymoon in Scotland, Hope was arrested and unmasked as James Hatfield, a swindler and bigamist. In the midst of the ensuing uproar, Hatfield seems to have coolly bluffed his way onto a fishing trip and escaped across the lake. He was captured, two months later, in Wales and tried in Carlisle. Widespread public sympathy for Mary, who by then was with child, resulted in Hatfield's execution by hanging in 1803.

The story of the 'Keswick Imposter' became the currency of novelists and playwrights for the next century. Charles Lamb reported seeing a highly coloured version of the affair upon the London stage.

Mary later married a local farmer and she now lies buried in Caldbeck churchyard.

2 The Buttermere Tunnel

George Benson, the nineteenth-century owner of nearby Hassness House, is credited with the creation of this unusual feature. There are two theories why he had the tunnel built; one states that he was irritated at not being able to walk the entire circumference of the lake upon the shore; the other suggests that he had the tunnel blasted through the rocks to keep his workmen busy during idle winter months.

Group of conifers just south of Burtness Wood by the shores of Buttermere

RYDAL WATER

STARTING AND FINISHING
POINT
NPA car park at Pelter Bridge, along a
small lane just off the A591
(SE-364062)
LENGTH
$3\frac{3}{4}$ miles (6 km)
ASCENT
250 ft (75 m)

An attractive, reedy lake, all too easily passed by those hurrying along the road in search of the delights of Grasmere. The southern shore is the special preserve of the walker. A complete circuit—using the old coffin track between Town End and Rydal Mount—makes a very enjoyable family walk.

ROUTE DESCRIPTION (Map 4)

From the car park turn L along the minor road, following the lane uphill, past two tiny rows of terraced cottages. After 400 yards (364 m) you pass through a gap alongside a farm gate and the lane deteriorates to a muddy track. The route descends to another farm gate. Go through the small gate alongside and you find yourself beside Rydal Water.

The path forks as soon as you come through the gate. The R-hand path takes you down to the lake and a route which meanders along the lake shore. Go L, uphill to a small wooden bench and a good view over the lake. Directly in front of you, on the far side of the lake, is Nab Scar and below the crag, by the road, is a white cottage *(1)*.

Continue along the path, crossing a small beck and bearing L to climb up into the trees. As the stone wall on your right gives out, you can detour L slightly to avoid a stretch of rough ground. Then bear R again (beware a faint track off to your L, through the bracken) to join the track where the wall resumes. Continue uphill to an old slate quarry. You will pass a cave on your L. Although safe to explore, there is quite a scramble to enter it.

Follow the path past the cave and you start to climb a steep-sided slate tip. This brings you out onto a wide plateau and, in front of you, another, larger cave *(2)*.

Bear R across the plateau and over a small incline, disregarding a path on your L. Passing another bench, you walk downhill again along a clearly defined path. Ahead of you is White Moss Common. Bear around to the L of a group of conifers, following the bracken-covered flanks of Loughrigg Fell.

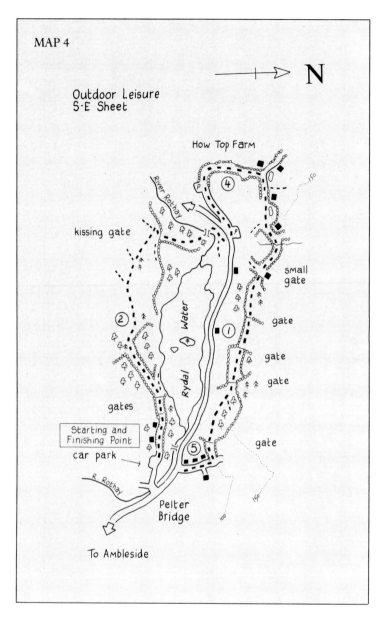

MAP 4

Outdoor Leisure
S-E Sheet

N

How Top Farm

River Rothay

kissing gate

4

P

150

small gate

gate

Rydal Water

2

1

gate

gate

gate

gates

Starting and Finishing Point

car park →

5

R. Rothay

Pelter Bridge

150

100

To Ambleside

Just beyond the trees, the path forks, the L-hand path taking you up onto Loughrigg Terrace. Bear half-R and follow the path up onto a small ridge, overlooking the river which links Grasmere Lake and Rydal Water. Ahead of you, across Grasmere, is Helm Crag (3).

At the ridge, turn R and follow the path downhill to a kissing gate in the stone wall on your L. Go through and you are in a pleasant, mixed woodland. The path is heavily eroded and

Rydal Water used to be called Routhermere or Rothaymere after the river which flows through it

therefore easy to follow. It winds downhill through the trees and brings you to a long wooden footbridge across the river. Once you have crossed, turn R and follow the river until you arrive at a fork in the path. Bear L and the path climbs uphill to the main road.

Cross the road and bear L through White Moss car park. There is a road ahead of you which goes up onto White Moss Common—and, invariably, in summer an ice cream van standing at the junction of this minor road and the A591. Follow the minor road uphill.

Follow the road for perhaps a $\frac{1}{3}$ mile (0.5 km) and you will pass a grove of trees on your R. There is a path which detours through the tree to a wooden bench and a grand view of Grasmere Lake (4) before rejoining the road a few hundred yards farther on.

Continue along the road until the junction at How Top Farm. Turn R (there is a slate sign by the road marked 'Footpath to Rydal') and continue up the hill, passing a sign on your L for Alcock Tarn. The road continues past a small pond and then peters out to a rough track. Ignore the path on your R which climbs over White Moss Common. The track winds round to the R, over Dunney Beck and passes just below a house called Brockstone. Once again, ignore a footpath on your R and continue through a small gate and along the track.

The track can be rough in places but it is straightforward walking. You follow the line of the wall on your R, past a stone embankment in the fellside, and through another gate in the stone wall on your R. This takes you through trees with glimpses of scree on the fellside above you. After 300 yards (273 m), you pass through another gate in a stone wall ahead of you and walk across a succession of fields, keeping to the clearly-defined track the whole time. On your right you start to have a clear view over Rydal Water.

After $\frac{1}{2}$ mile (0.8 km) you pass through a farm gate and the track leads between two stone walls to emerge onto a tarmac road. Turn R and walk downhill, past Rydal Mount (5).

This quiet lane leads down to the A591 again. Turn L and follow the road for 300 yards (273 m) until you come opposite Peler Bridge. Cross the road and walk back to the car park.

1 Nab Cottage

Originally Nab Farm, this house was the home of Margaret Simpson who was courted and later married by Thomas De Quincey. In 1829 he bought the house from her father and moved to the farm.

De Quincey first came to the Lake District in 1805,

making a pilgrimage to see his great idol, Wordsworth. His nerve failed him, however, and he returned to university at Oxford, having only got as far as Coniston. In April the following year, he tried again; the following August he actually got close enough to see Dove Cottage! He finally made it in 1807, accompanying Coleridge's wife, Sara, on the long journey from the West Country to Grasmere. He stayed several months and when Wordsworth moved to Allan Bank, he took over the tenancy.

It was here that he achieved notoriety as the author of *Confessions of an English Opium Eater*, first published in *London Magazine* in 1821. Even before this time, Wordsworth seems to have treated him badly, even writing to De Quincey's mother to urge her to put a stop to this unsuitable liaison with a farmer's daughter. De Quincey kept on the tenancy of Dove Cottage for ten years after moving to the Nab, mainly to store his vast wealth of books. He later got his own back on Wordsworth and his circle with a wonderful collection of scurrilous memories, entitled *Recollections of the Lakes and the Lake Poets*.

2 Rydal Caves

These caves—caused by slate quarrying—have now become an accepted feature of the local landscape. The second of them is the larger—the roof is nearly 40 feet (12 m) high— and has served over the years as picnic site, rain shelter, camp site and even concert hall; students from Charlotte Mason College in Ambleside frequently sing carols here just prior to the Christmas vacation.

3 Helm Crag

This craggy summit stands to the north of the village and is known variously as 'The Lion and the Lamb' and 'The Old Woman on the Organ', because of the fantastic shapes which are formed by the rocks on the summit. One nineteenth-century writer was so impressed that he even claimed that Helm Crag was the shell of an extinct volcano.

4 John's Grove

William and Dorothy Wordsworth had their own pet names for much of the landscape around Grasmere and Rydal. One such was John's Grove, the short stretch of woodland which commands such a fine view of the lake and island. They named it after their brother, John, a captain in the merchant navy, who would sometimes pace up and down this grove, as if on the deck of his ship. He died when his ship, *The Earl of Abergavenny* went down off Portland Bill in storms in 1805. Over 300 crew and passengers perished and the newspapers of the day regarded it as a national catastrophe.

Cave near Rydal Water

5 *Rydal Mount*

Wordsworth's home from 1813 until his death in 1850. He moved here to escape the unhappy associations of Grasmere vale, following the deaths of his two youngest children. By this time, Wordsworth was past his best as a poet and the radical reformer of his youth had given way to a somewhat staid member of the establishment of the day. He became a kind of civil servant—Distributor of Stamps for Westmorland—and, in 1843, was appointed Poet Laureate, following the death of his old friend, Robert Southey. A much grander house than Dove Cottage, it became a popular tourist attraction, even during the poet's lifetime. The house is now open to the public. (See Appendix for address and telephone number.)

A short distance down the road is the Church of St Mary, built by Lady Ann Fleming (Wordsworth's landlady) in 1824. Wordsworth was chapel warden in 1833. Behind the church lies Dora's Field, now owned by the National Trust. It was originally purchased by Wordsworth with the intention of building a home there, should he ever leave Rydal Mount (Wordsworth did not own any of the houses he lived in). He eventually gave it to his daughter, Dora, and each Spring it boasts a beautiful display of daffodils.

1·5

CASTLE CRAG

STARTING AND FINISHING
POINT
Car park along the lane opposite
Rosthwaite post office (NW-257148)
LENGTH
3 miles (4.8 km)
ASCENT
660 ft (200 m)

Castle Crag is the rocky, tree-lined emminence that stands at the Jaws of Borrowdale, guarding the entrance to the valley. Perhaps for this reason, it was chosen as a hill fort over 2,000 years ago. It stands at one of the most beautiful parts of the Lake District, with wonderful views all round, making this an ideal objective for a moderate family walk.

ROUTE DESCRIPTION (Map 5)

Upon leaving the car park by the main entrance, turn R and walk along the little lane, past a number of attractive stone cottages. When you come to Yew Tree Farm, bear R (signed: 'Footpath to Grange') and you find yourself walking along a well-made bridleway, between two stone walls with fields on either side. High Scawdale lies in front of you with Tongue Gill forming a distinctive gash in the fellside.

After a $\frac{1}{4}$ mile (0.4 km), the track brings you to the River Derwent. The track bears R and follows the riverbank but an alternative is to cross the river via the stepping stones and, once on the other side, turn R through a small wooden gate (beside a farm gate which says: No Admittance). This path takes you along the far bank, through trees, but can be very muddy in winter. The path crosses two small footbridges (ignore the stile in the fence on your L as you come off the first bridge). As you walk onto the second bridge, notice the slate gate post which is used as a step. Once over the second footbridge, go through a small gate and rejoin the main track as it crosses the river via New Bridge.

Continue straight ahead, the track leading past a small enclosure on your R, rich in wild flowers. The track brings you to a pair of farm gates. Cross the stile beside the R-hand gate and continue across the field. The river is lovely and clear and it is quite easy to spot fish as you follow the riverbank. This is an excellent part of the walk for an early morning stroll when everything is fresh and bright and you are still feeling smug about getting up early.

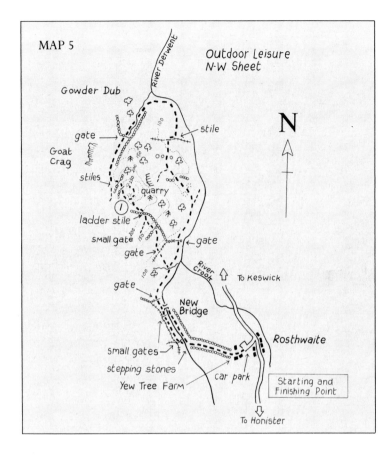

MAP 5

Outdoor Leisure
N-W Sheet

River Derwent

Gowder Dub

gate

Goat
Crag

stiles

quarry

ladder stile

small gate

gate

gate

N

stile

River Crook

gate

New
Bridge

To Keswick

Rosthwaite

small gates

stepping stones

Yew Tree Farm

car park

Starting and
Finishing Point

To Honister

Three hundred yards (273 m) from the gates, the track crosses a small stream and bears L around a wooded knoll, leaving the river away to your R. Once past the knoll, the track curves to the R again and follows a wire fence to bring you to a farm gate and a kissing gate. This leads you into High Hows Wood.

You are now on a narrower path, meandering through a pleasant, mixed woodland. You can occasionally glimpse the river to your R, through the trees. You pass a steep crag on your L whereupon the footpath forks. Keep half-L and you emerge from the trees into a clearing on the edge of a quarry. Walk through the quarry, bearing half-R past a pair of slate cairns and through a gap in the stone wall which crosses the path. You start to climb uphill, the path becoming rough and strewn with slate. Once past a large slate tip on your L you are out of the quarry and ascending steeply into the trees.

Within a short distance you arrive at a junction in the path. L is the old quarry track and is not recommended. Instead, go R (look for two yellow arrows on a sign, waymarking the route)

Borrowdale from Castle Crag

and begin to go downhill through the trees. The path crosses a broken stone wall and bears R, to follow the wall for a short distance. It then bears away from the wall, crossing a small beck and descending to a grassy clearing.

You arrive at an attractive glade and the path quickly rejoins the river to form a lovely route along the riverbank. After 200 yards (182 m), the path leads into the trees again, leaving the river below, but still in view. This gives a very pleasant vantage point from which to look down at the broad bend in the river—a favourite spot for swimmers and picnickers.

At the top of the hill you will encounter a wire fence. Cross by the stile and walk downhill again to Gowder Dub, the small stream below you. Do not cross, but turn L (PBS Seatoller, Honister) and head upstream. You now find yourself on a broad stone track which goes slowly uphill, running alongside an old, moss-covered stone wall on your L. After 200 yards (182 m), the track crosses the stream and continues into the trees. This is an old packhorse route—notice how it has been carefully engineered to prevent the horses' hooves from slipping.

One hundred yards (90 m) beyond the stream, you come to a farm gate in a stone wall and once through you have open fellside on your R with an impressive cliff—Goat Crag—towering above you. The track runs past massive slate screes on your L and begins to become indistinct just as you arrive at a large cairn. At the cairn, bear half-L (do not cross the beck just beyond this point) onto a faint footpath which runs behind a rock outcrop and climbs to a stone wall. Cross the stile (note the hog-hole just on your left) and, 20 yards (18 m) from the wall, you resume walking along an obvious route, climbing rapidly uphill. You pass a seat on your R, beneath a yew tree.

Continue to zigzag steeply uphill until you come to another stone wall. In fact, this is more of an embankment and once you ascend the ladder stile you realise that the fell on the other side is level with the top of the wall. Turn R and then immediately L, crossing a wire fence via a wooden stile. Turn R again and follow the fence until it peters out and the footpath is in front of you once more.

The footpath now climbs up the dramatic slate tip on your L. The path is perfectly safe and easy to follow, albeit very hard work at times. It can be loose underfoot in places, so care must be taken. It is easy to underestimate Castle Crag and end up attempting this part of the route in unsuitable footwear.

The path climbs to a slate cairn and splits two ways; the path R runs across the fellside to a stone wall and a ladder stile—this returns you to Rosthwaite but for now turn L and continue climbing to the summit (take heart—it is not far).

River Derwent

You arrive on a grassy, tree-lined plateau with superb views of Derwentwater and Borrowdale. *(1)*.

From the summit, retrace the route back to the last slate cairn and turn L, to follow the path across to the stone wall and ladder stile. Ten yards (9 m) beyond the wall, the path splits again. Go L and the path winds steeply downhill across a grass-covered fellside (from May onwards look out for the bright yellow petals of tormentil around here). After 300 yards (273 m) you come across a stone wall cutting across in front of you; go through a small gate and continue downhill, back into trees. The path is badly eroded in places. Once you emerge from the trees, there is a short descent across a field to a farm gate. Go through and you rejoin the outgoing path, just before the entrance to High Hows Wood. Turn R and retrace the route to the village (perhaps this time varying your route slightly to walk over New Bridge and return along the east bank of the River Derwent).

1 Castle Crag summit

The memorial on the summit of Castle Crag commemorates John Hamer, killed in action in 1918. Castle Crag itself was given to the National Trust in 1920, by John's father, Sir William Hamer. A seat, lower down on the walk, is a memorial to Sir William.

1·6

ALCOCK TARN

STARTING AND FINISHING
POINT
Grasmere village. Park at the NPA car
park in Broadgate (SE-337077).
LENGTH
3½ miles (5.6 km)
ASCENT
990 feet (300 m)

No one could possibly claim that Alcock Tarn is the most
beautiful stretch of water in the Lake District; nor is it the
largest or the most spectacularly sited. For reasons such as
these, this route is neglected by many who walk the fells around
Grasmere. This is a shame, for as you continue a little beyond
the tarn onto Butter Crag, you have a splendid panorama of the
head of Grasmere valley.

ROUTE DESCRIPTION (Map 6)

Directly opposite the car park entrance, there is a wooden
footbridge which crosses the River Rothay (PFS 'riverside path').
Cross the bridge and follow the broad footpath along a field
boundary, winding around behind the houses. At a point where
the footpath is intersected by a wide track, continue straight
across (following the 'riverside path' sign again) and you will
find yourself walking along the riverbank. Follow the path
around the fields until you emerge onto the road beside St
Oswald's Church *(1)*.

Turn L and go through the churchyard. Once back on the
road, turn L again and follow the road back towards the A591.
At the junction, go straight across and along a narrow lane
directly in front of you. This takes you into Town End; after a
few yards you cannot fail to notice that you are passing Dove
Cottage on your left *(2)*.

Continue uphill, past the houses and keep a close eye on the
stone wall on your L; as it ends, notice the large, flat-topped
boulder *(3)*. Follow the road past the small pond until you come
to the junction at How Top Farm. Turn L and follow the road
for 100 yards (91 m) until you come to a bench and a path off to
your L (PFS 'Alcock Tarn'). Turn L and follow the path uphill
and into the trees. Shortly past a gateway for Wood Close, on
your L, the path forks; keep R, past a National Trust sign for
'Brackenfell'. The path becomes steep and rough. You climb up
to a kissing gate. Go through and keep to the path bearing along
the stone wall on your L. You begin to ascend between two

stone walls and eventually reach a point at which there is a small metal gate on either side of you. Do not go through either of them, but if you look to your L you get an excellent view of Helm Crag. Keep climbing and as the path flattens out towards Grey Crag look out for a metal gate in the wall on your L. Cross via the stile alongside and follow the path across a beck to Alcock Tarn.

Not the most spectacular tarn that Lakeland has to offer—in fact, it is part-artificial. Tucked away behind Grey Crag it is isolated from the views in a secluded fold in the fellside. Follow the footpath past the tarn and cross the stile at the far end. The path continues directly ahead, skirting an area of bog and running alongside a stone wall on your L. As you leave the wall and pass a large cairn you can see Greenhead Gill ahead of you. A few yards farther on you come out onto a rocky outcrop at Butter Crag and a glorious view of Grasmere valley. The panorama hits you unexpectedly and makes the steep climb to Alcock Tarn worthwhile. From this point you can see well up into Easedale (though not the tarn itself, unfortunately) and beyond that to Sergeant Man, Great Gable and the Scafell range.

Looking towards Grasmere during the ascent to Alcock Tarn

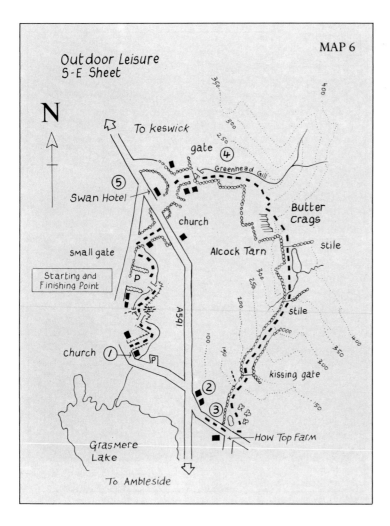

MAP 6

Outdoor Leisure
5-E Sheet

N

To Keswick

gate

④

Greenhead Gill

⑤

Swan Hotel

Butter
Crags

church

stile

Alcock Tarn

small gate

Starting and
Finishing Point

P

stile

A591

church

①

kissing gate

P

②

③

How Top Farm

Grasmere
Lake

To Ambleside

When you are ready, continue past the crags, bearing slightly to the L and descending steeply in a series of broad zigzags. Disregard the occasional sheep track which comes in from the side. The path drops very quickly to the gill, arriving at a stone wall on your L. Follow the wall down to the gill *(4)* and then turn L and follow the beck downhill. After 200 yards (182 m) you will reach a footbridge. Cross the beck and go through the farm gate in the wall on your L. This brings you onto a rough track which you should follow downhill until you emerge onto a peaceful minor road. Turn L and follow the lane until you meet the A591, arriving next to the Swan Hotel *(5)*.

Turn L along the road for 100 yards (91 m) until you come to Our Lady of the Wayside Church. Cross the road at this point and in the wall on the other side you will find a clearly defined footpath, running between two fields (signed: Pedestrians only).

Grasmere village and Helm Crag from Butter Crag

Go down the path and follow it across the fields to the village. You come back onto Broadgate; turn L and follow the road until you path the Rothay Garden Hotel on your L. Then turn L, through a small wooden gate and follow the path around the park to rejoin the river. Turn R along the bank and the path takes you straight back into the car park.

1 St Oswald's Church

Grasmere Church dates back to the thirteenth century and is today most famous as the resting place of William Wordsworth. Inside the church itself there is a memorial to the poet, but it is the grave—in the north-east corner of the little churchyard—which attracts the crowds. He lies here with his sister, Dorothy, wife, Mary, and other members of his family. Alongside is the grave of Hartley, son of Samuel Taylor Coleridge.

St Oswald's remains one of the few churches in the Lake District to conduct an annual rushbearing service. This ancient ceremony commemorates the day when the old rushes were removed and the church floor strewn with new. Today, the ceremony is enacted by a small procession of children from the village; the girls wear crowns of flowers and the boys carry crosses made from rushes.

Rushbearing ceremonies can also be seen at Ambleside, Urswick, Musgrave and Warcop—always between late June and early August. In addition to Grasmere, the Warcop rushbearing is particularly worth trying to see.

2 Dove Cottage

Dove Cottage was originally built as an inn, the *Dove and Olive Branch*, sometime around the early seventeenth century. In 1799, it became the home of William and Dorothy Wordsworth, who rented it from a local farmer for £5 a year (plus an additional 7 shillings annual window tax, which one wag of the period described as daylight robbery). William married in 1802 and had three children at the cottage. His wife's sister, Sarah Hutchinson, also lived with the family and, by 1808 the house was becoming rather crowded. They moved across the valley to a newly-built house called Allan Bank.

The early, day-to-day life of the Wordsworths, with its simple philosophy of 'plain living and high thinking', was recorded by Dorothy in her journal. The poetry William produced whilst living here includes some of his best and most well-loved work.

The house was first opened to the public in 1899, having been bought by the Dove Cottage Trust, which still maintains it to this day. It has been furnished with much of William's original furniture and visitors receive a guided tour of the house and grounds. On a quiet morning, before the crowds arrive, it is sometimes possible to wander around by yourself and get a sense of what it must have been like in Wordsworth's time.

Next door to the cottage there is a modern museum which, in addition to telling the story of Wordsworth's life and work, features a number of special exhibitions throughout the year, related either to the area or the period in which Wordsworth lived. The Trust also runs a bookshop and a newly-acquired restaurant.

3 *The Coffin Stone*

This flat-topped boulder, just above Town End, stands on the old coffin track to Rydal. The dead were brought along this route on their way to Rydal church, Grasmere at that time having no churchyard of its own. The bearers would rest their load on this stone before continuing along the track; hence its name—Coffin Stone.

4 *Greenhead Gill*

Greenhead Gill was the setting of one of Wordsworth's best-known poems, *Michael*. Written whilst the poet lived at Dove Cottage, it sets Wordsworth's ideals of the nobility of the statesman farmer against the worldliness of the city-dweller. It tells the tale of a shepherd's son leaving the valley for the city, to redeem his father's estate.

5 *The Swan Hotel*

Originally the Swan Inn, this establishment had its part to play in the life of Wordsworth. It was during a visit to Wordsworth, in 1805, that the poet and novelist, Walter Scott grew into the habit of frequenting the Swan Inn for breakfast. Objecting to the monotonous diet of porridge at Dove Cottage, he used to sneak out of his bedroom window, whilst the rest of the household thought he was still asleep, and repair to the Swan for something more substantial.

CAT BELLS

STARTING AND FINISHING
POINT
Launch from Keswick to the pier at
Hawes End (NW-252213).
Alternatively, you can start from
Gutherscale car park (NW-247212),
thereby cutting out the trip on
Derwent Water. (Note that the
launches run alternately clockwise
and anti-clockwise around the lake;
the anti-clockwise trip is the quickest
to Hawes End, lasting about ten
minutes.)
LENGTH
4 miles (6.4 km)
ASCENT
1255 ft (380 m)

Cat Bells—the delightful name derives from the wild cats which once roamed this district. This prominent, hump-backed ridge to the west of Derwent Water must be one of the most popular routes in the Keswick area. The views are splendid and the stiff climb onto the ridge gives you a fine sense of accomplishment. For the complete experience, catch one of the Keswick launches to Hawes End in order to begin the walk. The return route brings you back to the jetty through a delightful National Trust woodland on the shore of Derwent Water.

ROUTE DESCRIPTION (Map 7)

Disembark at Hawes End onto a rickety, wooden landing stage. Walk straight up the beach and into the trees to join a footpath. Turn R, to cross a footbridge then R again at the fork in the path. This brings you to a kissing gate. Go through onto a cart-track and turn R for a few yards, then L and through another kissing gate, into a small conifer wood. By now your ears should have recovered from the racket of the launch trip. The path climbs though the wood to join the Portinscale road.

Follow the road uphill, over the cattle grid, until you come to a junction. Turn L (signed: 'Grange $2\frac{1}{2}$') and follow the road for 100 yards (91 m) until you come to a footpath on your R. Leave the road and start to climb the side of Cat Bells. Follow any diversion signs you may encounter if footpath maintenance work is in progress.

The path zigzags uphill very steeply but after a short distance you begin to get a good view over the lake. This provides you with an excellent excuse to stop now and then to catch your breath. The footpath becomes rough and loose in places as it climbs sharply towards the top. Just below the summit you scramble up a rocky outcrop; look out for a slate plaque mounted in the rock (1).

Once you have attained the summit, you have a superb panorama of Newlands Valley and the northern fells. The route along the ridge is obvious.

Opposite Derwent Water and Skiddaw from Cat Bells (note erosion—this is a very popular route)

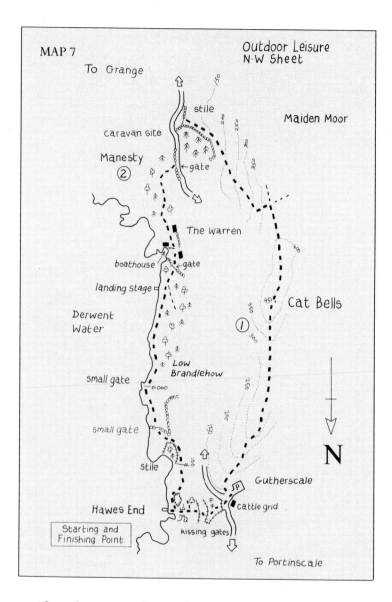

After almost a mile of splendid ridge walking, the path descends to a wide, flat area with Maiden Moor looming ahead. At the junction of tracks, turn L and begin a steep descent down a series of step-like terraces. The path is well-laid and follows a broad zigzag pattern until it begins to level off as you draw close to a group of larches. Ignoring any incoming paths, follow the track down to a stile in a stone wall. From this point you have an excellent view of the Jaws of Borrowdale.

Cross the stile and join the road. Turn L and follow the road, past Low Manesty caravan site, until you come to a farm gate in the wall on your R (signed: 'NT Manesty Woods'). Turn R and follow the track through the woods *(2)*.

After a ¼ mile (0.4 km), the track leads you to a small bay

Approaching the summit of Cat Bells

beside the lake. You pass a slate house, called The Warren, and 200 yards (182 m) farther on come to a fork in the path, beside a boathouse. Go L to pass a small bungalow and the path then bears R, through a stone wall and back into the trees. Take the R-hand path at the next fork and you find yourself on a very attractive woodland route along the shores of Derwent Water.

Continue along the shore, through a kissing gate at Low Brandlehow, and across a field. As you come within sight of Hawes End jetty, the path leaves the shore to divert around a bed of reeds and you encounter a strange, curved bench, following the line of the fence. This is actually a walk-way, as the path suffers from frequent flooding in winter.

Beyond the reeds, you take the lower path across a field to arrive at a stile. Cross and continue through the woods back to the jetty.

1 *Memorial Plaque*
  This is a memorial to Thomas Arthur Leonard, 'founder of Co-Operative and Communal Holidays and "father" of the open-air movement in this country'. Leonard was born in 1864 and, whilst a minister in Lancashire, founded the Co-Operative Holidays Association, in 1892. This organization was the direct forerunner of the Countrywide Holidays Association. It sought to provide houses and residences— either leased or bought—for its members. The CHA thrives to this day. (See address in Appendix.)
2 *Manesty Woods*
  A very old woodland originally purchased by the National Trust in 1908. The first property in the Lake District ever bought by the Trust lies at the northern end of this walk; Brandlehow Park, acquired in 1902.

Muncaster Fell

STARTING AND FINISHING
POINT
Park in the tiny car park at The Green
station (SW-146998) and catch the
miniature railway to Ravenglass
station. The walk begins at Ravenglass
and ends at The Green.
LENGTH
5¼ miles (8.4 km)
ASCENT
677 ft (205 m) (slightly more if you
detour to the summit)

The summit of Muncaster Fell is the route of an ancient road, probably once used by the Romans and latterly a carriage way for the estates of Muncaster Castle. Today, Fell Road makes a superb walk between the pastures of Miterdale and the lower reaches of Eskdale. It may only be 757 feet high (231 m) but it offers a wonderful panorama both seawards and inwards, to the fells of central Lakeland. The ideal way to begin this walk is with a journey on the Ravenglass and Eskdale Railway, beginning at Eskdale Green and arriving at Ravenglass to begin a memorable walk.

ROUTE DESCRIPTION (Maps 8, 9)

From The Green take the train *(1)* to Ravenglass. This is a pleasant journey through verdant countryside, running around the north-west flank of Muncaster Fell. Once at Ravenglass station, it is worth a short detour to investigate the village itself before beginning the walk *(2)*.

Walk to the end of the station platform, past the tiny turntable, and turn L, past a small group of picnic tables and into a grass-covered children's playground. Go L again and follow short path between two wire fences to emerge onto a tarmac lane alongside the main road. Turn R (PFS 'Walls Castle, Newtown Knott and Muncaster') and follow the lane, passing Walls Caravan and Camping Park on your L. After ½ mile (0.8 km) along a nice avenue of trees, you come to Walls Castle on your L *(3)*.

After much speculation on the richness of England's heritage, continue along the lane for a further 100 yards (91 m) until you reach a fork. The tramac track continues right and leads to Walls Mansion. Take the L-hand fork (PFS 'Newtown Cottage'). This track is rougher underfoot and takes you into the woods. After a few minutes, as the trees on your R start to thin out, you can catch glimpses of the sea and Eskmeal Dunes.

Descent to Eskdale Green from Muncaster Fell

Walls Castle, Ravenglass—the ancient bath house to the Dorian fort of Glannaventa

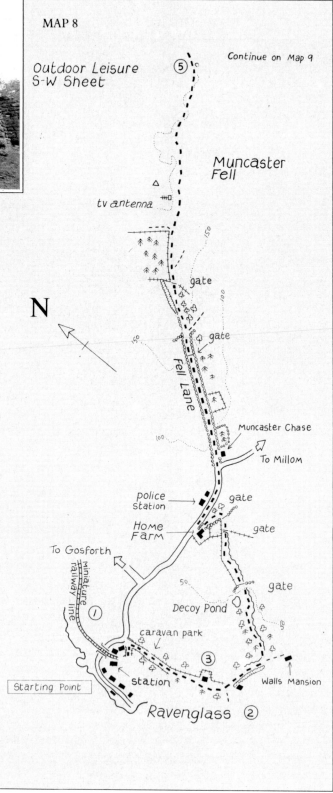

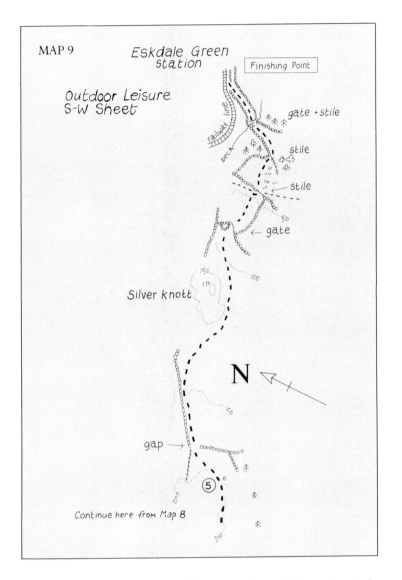

MAP 9 Eskdale Green station

Finishing Point

Outdoor Leisure S-W Sheet

railway line

beck

gate + stile

stile

stile

gate

Silver knott

N

gap →

⑤

Continue here from Map 8

This path can be quite muddy at the best of times. It winds through the trees and rhododendron bushes and after 400 yards (364 m) you come to a path on your L (signed, simply, 'footpath'). Go L and continue past Walls Plantation on your R. The overgrown beck on your L disappears after a while, to re-emerge on your R in a wide, shallow, densely-vegetated gorge.

Once past a rocky knoll and pond, surrounded by reeds, on your L, you arrive at a farm gate standing between two fine, if somewhat incongruous, stone gateposts. Once through, the path continues to follow the stream on your R and shortly you emerge from the trees to find fields on either side. Away to your R is a long, curving stone wall with woods beyond. This marks the boundary of Muncaster Castle grounds (4).

The path arrives at a wooden farm gate, with a stile alongside (ignore the gate in the wire fence on your L). 100 yards (91 m) further on, you come to another farm gate which leads into the small wood beside Home Farm. Once in the wood, the path bears L (if you continue straight ahead you are confronted by a gate bearing the words 'No Admittance'). After another 200 yards (182 m), you enter the farmyard itself. Walk past the buildings, keeping to the path, past a long red stone barn, and you come onto the main road (A595).

Cross to the pavement on the other side and turn R, following the road uphill, past the police station and a small guest house (once the local school). You will pass the entrance to Muncaster Castle on your R.

Continue along the road for a $\frac{1}{4}$ mile (0.4 km) until the road bears sharp R. Directly in front of you is a rough track (PBS Eskdale and Hardknott). Follow this track, past an old farmhouse called Muncaster Chase.

This rough track is called Fell Lane. As you start to climb uphill, the views behind you begin to open out and you can look back over Ravenglass to the sea. On a really clear day the Isle of Man is visible.

Fell Lane is an attractive, winding country lane, running alongside a small wood on your R. After a few hundred yards, look out for a clearing in the trees and you begin to get a good view of the valley below. Continue along the track, through an iron farm gate, and as the conifer wood on your R gives out, the track starts to bear round to the R.

You come to a junction in the track, where Fell Lane turns off R towards High Eskholme and Muncaster Head. Continue straight on, passing through a gate and emerging onto open fellside, with a small conifer plantation on your L.

Keep to the path, running alongside the plantation, and where it forks at the end of the trees, keep straight on.

Ahead of you lies an undulating, bracken-covered fellside. It is criss-crossed by muddy cart-tracks and wheel ruts. In the main, it is easy to distinguish and ignore these ruts. To begin with, you are heading directly towards the summit cairn and an oddly-placed television aerial. After a while, the path begins to bear to the R of the summit. As you come level with the TV aerial, it is worth detouring up the fellside to the trig point at the summit. This point gives you superb views out to the coast (Sellafield is just to the north), to Wasdale and, looking east, to the central fells of Lakeland. Not as bleak as the higher fells, Muncaster Fell has a wild, wind-swept air—nowhere in the Lake District do you feel closer to the Romans.

Returning to the path, continue beyond the summit, keeping to the path straight ahead. The path lies below the main ridge of

Muncaster Fell, keeping to the Eskdale side with good views down into the valley and the plain beyond, leading up to Birkby Fell. The path is wet and boggy in places, especially in winter, but for the most part is easy to follow. Eventually, $\frac{1}{2}$ mile (0.8 km) beyond the summit, you come across a large, flat rock, placed on a trio of supporting boulders. The rock is engraved 'Ross's Camp 1885' *(5)* and from here you can see down towards Eskdale Green village. Ahead of you lies Silver Knott. The path now works downhill a little, towards a drystone wall. Go through a gateway in the wall (no gate) and you find yourself in the corner of a rough, fellside field.

Once through the wall, the path descends quite quickly, following the wall at the outset. Once past a tiny row of young Silver Birch, you start to leave the stone wall away to your L as it circles round the opposite side of Silver Knott. The path winds up a short, stone embankment onto the southern flank of the hill, working uphill once more. The valley comes into view again and you can see Eskdale Green ahead of you.

The path levels out alongside Silver Knott before beginning a gentle, muddy descent. Once past the hill, the wall comes in again from your L and you bear half-R towards a sheep enclosure at the corner of the field. Unless it has been a long, dry summer, this patch can be very muddy. Pick your way across the quagmire and through a gate next to the sheep enclosure. The gorse-covered knoll directly ahead of you is Rabbit How. The path winds through the bushes to the R of the knoll before descending once more to a stone wall running across a field in front of you. Turn R for a few yards until you come to a stile and a farm gate.

Once over the stile, you are in a pasture field which drops away to your R to a rough marsh. At the stile is a junction of three paths and a footpath sign. Go L, following the contour of the field towards a copse of deciduous trees (this route signed: 'The Green and The Station'). As you cross the field there is a stone wall, enclosing a conifer plantation, on your L and ahead of you is a wire fence. Make your way towards the junction of the two, crossing the fence via a small wooden stile. Now bear L, following the stone wall on your L, until it brings you down to the corner of another field, where two stone walls meet. Go through a gap between the two walls and you have arrived at a rough track, crossed by a small beck. Turn half-R and walk a few yards to a farm gate and a stile. Continue uphill, between two stone walls, the track bearing round to the L. The track is overgrown and can be muddy, but after 200 yards (182 m) or so you begin to detect signs of civilization on your L, in the shape of houses and, eventually, the miniature railway line. Continue along the track until it meets a gap in the wall on your L and a sign which reads: 'Danger—trains. Please cross here'. Go through the gap and turn R, without crossing the line, and you find yourself back on the platform of Eskdale Green station.

1 The Ravenglass and Eskdale Railway

La'al Ratty, as it is known locally, has had a long and chequered career. Originally opened in 1875, its purpose was to carry iron ore from the mines at Boot down to the main line at Drigg. It was built at a total cost of £42,000 and had an immediate effect on the price of ore, which fell from ten shillings to two shillings per ton. Passenger services began in 1876 and became the main source of income when the mines failed in 1882. It closed down in 1908, but re-opened in 1909 as the Eskdale Railway Company. It lasted four years. Then, in 1915, Narrow Gauge Railways Limited re-opened the line and the Dalegarth terminus was opened in 1920.

With the re-opening of the quarries at Beckfoot, the line was purchased by the Keswick Granite Company in 1949, but they put it up for sale again, nine years later.

Finally, in 1960, it was bought by the Ravenglass and Eskdale Preservation Society for the grand sum of £12,000. Since then, its success has grown until it is now one of the area's most popular attractions. Although the major source of its income remains the visitor, it still serves a purpose as a 'commuter' link with the main line at Ravenglass. For this reason, it runs throughout the winter.

2 Ravenglass

Ravenglass was once an important port, stretching back to Saxon and Roman times. The Romans built a fort here—Glannaventa—but it was largely destroyed by the Victorians, to make way for the main line railway along the Cumbrian coast. With the silting of the estuary, Ravenglass lost its former importance and now remains a quiet, largely unspoilt village. At the end of the main street is access to the sands and Eskmeal Dunes Nature Reserve.

3 Walls Castle

This unprepossessing structure is the largest standing Roman building in the north of England. It was the bath house for Glannaventa and presumably escaped the ravages of the Victorians by being separated from the remains of the main settlement. A glass screen should be erected over it to save it from further erosion and damage.

Eskdale from Muncaster Fell, looking towards the coast with Birkby and Corney Fell in the distance

Two of the Ravenglass and Eskdale Railway's steam locomotives

4 *Muncaster Castle*

In common with the majority of Cumbrian castles, Muncaster Castle began life originally as a pele tower, in this case built around 1325. It has been the ancestral home of the Pennington family ever since. In the 1860s, the fourth Lord Muncaster commissioned Anthony Salvin to convert it into a comfortable and attractive mansion. Now open to the public (during the summer months only), the house contains some fascinating furniture and includes paintings by Reynolds and Gainsborough. The grounds themselves are magnificent in early summer when the rhododendrons and azaleas are at their best—spectacular when viewed against the backdrop of the Lakeland Fells. Perhaps slightly less in keeping with its historic background, the grounds also boast an exotic bird garden and a pair of wallabies. At least it keeps the children quiet whilst you explore the house.

Further details of Muncaster Castle can be obtained by ringing Ravenglass (065 77) 614.

5 *Ross's Camp*

Although Fell Lane is of Roman origin, Ross's Camp almost certainly isn't. Theories differ as to its origins—one suggests that it may have been a shelter for workmen working on the carriage road which once followed this route from Home Farm; another that it may have been built as a 'luncheon table' for a shooting party. Either way, it would not be the first time that a Victorian folly has found its way onto an OS map . . .

2·9

WATENDLATH

STARTING AND FINISHING
POINT
Rosthwaite village. There is a small
car park just along the lane, opposite
Rosthwaite post office (NW-257148).
LENGTH
$4\frac{1}{2}$ miles (7.2 km)
ASCENT
1255 ft (380 m)

Watendlath village was the home of Hugh Walpole's fictional heroine, Judith Paris. Its isolated and wind-swept setting must have seemed an ideal match for her tempestuous nature. This walk follows the popular ascent from Rosthwaite village and continues across open moorland to Dock Tarn.

ROUTE DESCRIPTION (Map 10)

Walk back along the lane to the village and turn L along the main road. After 30 yards (27 m) you come to a junction; turn R (signed: 'Hazel Bank Hotel') and follow the lane until you cross over Stonethwaite Beck. Once over the bridge, turn L onto a track which leads between two fields. After 200 yards (182 m) you cross a beck via a concrete ramp and immediately turn R, through a farm gate and onto a bridleway. This leads gently uphill and the fellside opens up with a gill to your R. Shortly, you come to another junction; the path L doubles back downhill and follows a fence, so keep R and continue gradually uphill, past a group of larch and rowan trees.

After a further 200 yards (182 m), the path winds steeply up to a well-marked footpath and you come to a gap in a stone wall on your L. Go through the gap and follow the clearly-defined path across the fell, towards a small conifer wood; you pass beneath Yew Crag on your R. Upon reaching the next stone wall, the footpath flattens out and you have an excellent view across the valley to Johnny's Wood. Cross the wall and you come to a beck. Go over the footbridge and bear upstream, keeping a stone wall on your L. Ignore the path on your L, signed 'Keswick and Bowder Stone', and continue uphill, past a group of Scots Pine. The path keeps to the L of a deep gorge until you reach a footbridge, whereupon you should cross over the gill and continue uphill, leaving the stream behind you.

As you climb up to Puddingstone Bank, you encounter a stone wall, which you should cross via a stile alongside a gate. The path then runs alongside a damp, marshy area to your R. Shortly after this, Watendlath Tarn comes into view and you start to bear steeply downhill across a boulder-strewn path. This brings you to a gate in a stone wall. Turn L through the gate and continue downhill to cross a small packhorse bridge. Turn R and enter the village *(1)*.

After exploring this small group of houses (and, perhaps more vital, exploring the teashop), retrace your steps over the packhorse bridge and bear around the lake shore, through a gate (PFS 'Dock Tarn') to another pair of gates. Go through the R-hand gate (marked 'Path') and follow the broad track across

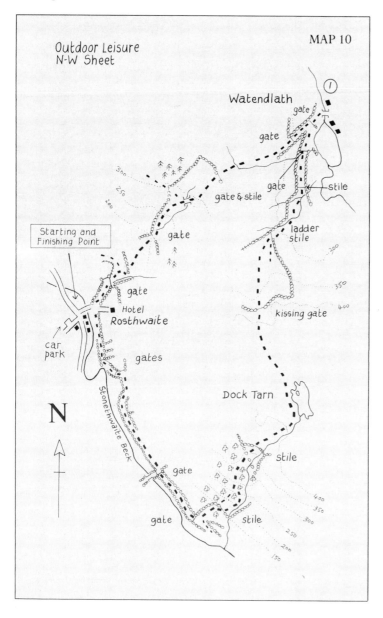

Rosthwaite and Borrowdale from the path to Watendlath

Watendlath Tarn

enclosed fields, leaving the tarn behind you on your L.

After 400 yards (364 m) you come to a small beck. Cross the stone stile and continue to follow the beck for a short distance until the path bears R, by an arrowed sign. Walk uphill until you come to another beck, then bear R and follow the beck uphill. You eventually lose the beck under the wall on your R. Follow the wall until it is met by another stone wall coming in from your L and cross via ladder stile. Go straight ahead, keeping to the wall until the path bears away to the L, 100 yards (91 m) from the stile.

The path bears across rough bracken and heather, past a sloping-topped boulder. This section of the walk can get very boggy at times. Heading almost due south, you come to a wall between two obvious crags. Go through the kissing gate and there is a steep, eroded path in front of you. The path flattens out again and there is a level path, marked by cairns, which leads towards Dock Tarn.

Follow the path around the west side of the tarn until you encounter the outlet beck, whereupon the path bears R, following more cairns. The view before you is magnificent as you start to descend; you look out across Glaramara to Sourmilk Gill and Gillercombe. Further to the R is Honister Quarry and Dales Head.

The path follows a deep ravine and drops to meet a stone wall. Cross via the stile and continue downhill through a ruined wall, passing a pair of ruined buildings on your right. The descent becomes steeper and rougher; take this section slowly and eventually you begin to drop through an oak wood. The path rejoins Willygrass Gill just below a waterfall. As you come to a stone wall, cross a stile and continue down towards the valley bottom. Just clear of the woods, you meet up with a walled track; turn R, through a farm gate and follow the path round to the L of a sheepfold.

At the next gate, turn R and head along the old road (known as Back o'Beck), running parallel with Stonethwaite Beck. At the next pair of gates, go through the lower one and continue along the track until you are within $\frac{1}{4}$ mile (0.4 km) of the village and encounter another pair of gates. Go through the L-hand gate and follow the path back over the river and into Rosthwaite.

1 Watendlath Village

Watendlath is so isolated that it is only in recent years that the tiny hamlet has enjoyed the benefits of being connected to the national grid. The villagers celebrated by illuminating a Christmas tree in the car park.

In 1984, a telephone cable was first laid up here, buried alongside the path which you have taken to approach the tarn.

Fold Head Farm, at the far end of the village, is famous as the fictional home of Judith Paris, the tempestuous heroine of the second of the *Herries Chronicles*, written by Hugh Walpole. All four novels in the series—*Rogue Herries, Judith Paris, The Fortress* and *Vanessa*—had a Lake District setting and Walpole himself bought a house beside Derwent Water where he lived from 1924 until his death in 1941. His house, Brackenburn, is now in private hands and not open to the public.

2·10

HAYSTACKS

STARTING AND FINISHING
POINT
Gatesgarth Farm; park on the
roadside, next to the beck
(NW-195150)
LENGTH
$4\frac{1}{2}$ miles (7.2 km)
ASCENT
1720 feet (520 m)

Haystacks is an attractive little summit; an easy romp on a hot summer's day with plenty of time to spare to find a little cafe in Keswick and relax, with the feeling of a walk well done. Do not bother with Fleetwith Pike—a minefield of intersecting tracks and ruts, courtesy of the Buttermere and Westmorland Green Slate Company. The descent via Warnscale Beck is far superior, a scenic stroll past a number of delightful cascades.

ROUTE DESCRIPTION (Map 11)

Gatesgarth Farm stands at the head of Buttermere Lake, beside the Honister Pass road. Between the entrance to the farm and the road bridge, there is a small gate (PBS 'Buttermere and Ennerdale'). Go through and follow the track past the farm, keeping to the river. The track goes through another gate and heads across the fields to a farm gate. Go through and bear slight R, following the river until you come to a pair of farm gates. Go half-L, past the farm gates (not through them—sign on the gates: Please keep to footpath) and walk along the edge of a field, leaving the river behind you. The lake comes into view on your R and ahead of you is Buttermere Fell, with a good view L to Haystacks and Warnscale. After 150 yards (136 m), you arrive at another farm gate in a fence in front of you. Carry on through the kissing gate alongside and continue across the fields. 'Buttermere' literally means 'the lake by the dairy pastures' and at this point on the walk, it is easy to see why.

As you draw closer to a stone wall, the path crosses Warnscale Beck by means of a wooden bridge. Go through the kissing gate in the wall ahead of you. The track now forks two ways (look out for a public footpath sign which, at the time of writing, was missing). R takes you along the lake shore, so instead bear half-L, up a series of steps. The path is quite steep and eroded in places, but has recently been subject to maintenance work; follow any footpath diversion signs and adjust your route with the aid of a map, where necessary. You start to gain height very quickly and soon have good views opening up behind you of the lake and village.

One hundred and fifty yards (136 m) beyond the wall, you will encounter a junction of several footpaths. Turn L so that you climb alongside a wire fence on your L. This fence marks the boundary of a young conifer plantation. A few yards farther on, the path crosses a beck via a small wooden bridge. Keep climbing; the footpath becomes very rough in places. Disregard a footpath joining you from the R, about 200 yards (182 m) up from the beck. As you climb, the route is marked by piles of stones which eventually lead you to a wire fence running across the path. Cross the stile and continue along a broad track, heading up into Scarth Gap. The rocky cliff on your right is High Crag.

The route follows a broken stone wall on your L and then begins to zigzag sharply to Scarth Gap. An old, broken wall comes down the fellside in front of you; as you approach, there

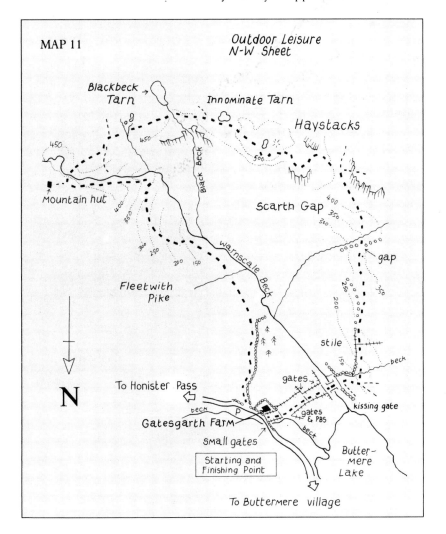

are so many boulders in the vicinity that it becomes difficult to follow the path. Look for a small cairn beside the wall and cross by the gap alongside. Cross a tiny beck and once across a further stretch of boulders you will see a line of stones stretching in front of you, marking the way.

The piles of stones lead you up through Scarth Gap and you arrive on a sloping, grassy hillside. Continue up the slope to a junction of four footpaths. From this point you can look down upon the conifer forests of Ennerdale and across to Pillar and Kirk Fell. On your R is Seat and the long ridge of High Stile and Red Pike. Turn L at the junction and begin the steep climb up the side of Haystacks. Once again, the going is rough underfoot in places and as you climb the path becomes indistinct in places; watch out for the piles of stones marking the route. Just below the summit, you have a short scramble up scree before arriving at a rock face. Bear L and the path takes you round the crag in a series of natural steps. On clear days you will start to get brilliant views out towards Cockermouth and the Solway Coast. The cone-shaped mountain on the horizon is Criffel, in Scotland. The path opens up onto a mossy fellside, dotted with heather and you get a magnificent view along the ridge to Red Pike.

Once on level ground, the path wanders along the eastern edge of the summit, forming a muddy little plateau before you come to the rocky summit itself.

The summit cairn stands to one side of a cleft in the rocks, with a tiny tarn formed below. It offers wonderful all-round views and the cleft itself provides good protection from the wind.

Continue past the cairn and follow an obvious path across the rocks towards a small, sheltered tarn below you. This is called Innominate Tarn, somewhat confusingly as its name means that it hasn't a name at all. The path bears L of the tarn and heads downhill across open fellside. This area acts as a good water table and so can be boggy in places almost all year round. Follow the footpath to pass Blackbeck Tarn; Black Beck itself drops away on your L through a dramatic cleft in the rocks, which gives you a good vantage point to look down to Buttermere.

As you walk across this wide, open moor, you can see Grey Knotts and Brandreth on your left and, on a busy afternoon, you will probably also see fellwalkers making their way towards Great Gable, just to the south of you.

Ahead of you are the Honister slate quarries, disfiguring Fleetwith Pike. Half a mile (0.8 km) or so beyond Blackbeck

Buttermere and Crummock Water from the summit of Haystacks

Quarry building above Warnscale Beck

Tarn, the path drops to Warnscale Beck.

The beck is quite wide and fast and drops away on your L in a series of waterfalls. Crossing the beck, bear L across muddy ground and go uphill a short distance to join a major track. If you turn R, this will take you past the mountain hut (known as 'The Ritz' by the grafitti on its door) and down to Honister Pass. At one time there was also a good alternative descent along the ridge of Fleetwith Pike, but in recent years the fellside has been so badly chewed up by the quarries that finding the path has become a difficult and tedious task.

Go L and follow the beck downstream. You pass a 15 foot (4.5 m) cascade on your L where the beck drops to a strikingly green pool before plunging into a dramatic gorge.

The path is a steep descent, the ground being rough and loose in places. There are odd rowan and gorse bushes dotted about, otherwise the fellside is harsh and rocky.

Once the path levels off at Warnscale Bottom, it becomes harder to distinguish and you have to follow the lines of stones. It winds through bracken and becomes a flat, easy route back towards the farm.

ULLSWATER

STARTING AND FINISHING
POINT
Park at Glenridding and catch the
launch to Howtown. The walk starts
from Howtown Pier (NE-444198) and
finishes back at Glenridding.
LENGTH
$6\frac{1}{2}$ miles (10.4 km)
ASCENT
395 ft (120 m)

The tree-lined eastern shores of Ullswater provide the setting
for this walk from Howtown to Glenridding. Undisturbed by
roads or traffic, this is one of the best low-level routes you will
encounter in the Lake District. The start of the walk is
approached by a launch from Glenridding, a very pleasant way
to survey the footpath before you begin.

ROUTE DESCRIPTION (Maps 12, 13)

Howtown stands beside a bay, overlooked by Hallin Fell and the
northern slopes of High Street. The launch *(1)* will tie alongside
a wooden pier which leads you into a group of trees and over a
tiny footbridge. Immediately you have crossed the beck, turn L
and go through a fence and along the lake shore. If you have
caught the first launch on a summer Sunday, you will have to
put on a burst of speed at this point to overtake the crowds.
Follow the shoreline around the bay and through a kissing gate.
At a second kissing gate, turn R along a farm track, continuing
along the shore. You will come to a farm gate and another
kissing gate (PFS 'Patterdale, Sandwick'). Go through, following
the stone wall on your R and up a series of steps to yet a further
kissing gate. Go through and turn R, following a clear track
around the side of Hallin Fell.

As you walk past the trees on your R, the view opens out and
you are looking across the bay and along Ullswater *(2)*. After $\frac{1}{2}$
mile (0.8 km), you have climbed perhaps 150 feet (45 m) above
the lake. You follow the path around Geordie's Crag and then it
descends again into the trees. You are now walking through
mixed, mainly deciduous woodland, right on the lake shore. The
path becomes rough underfoot in parts and brings you down
onto a rocky beach before re-entering the woods. You walk
around the L of a small wooded knoll and begin to climb again
along a well-made path through the trees, still keeping just
above the shoreline.

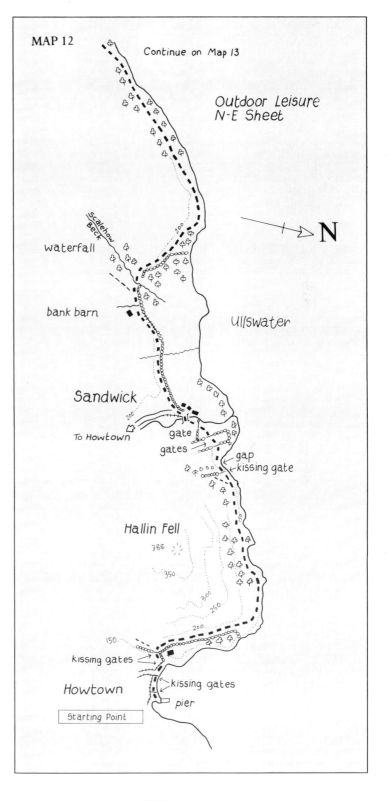

Near Sandwick on the shore of Ullswater

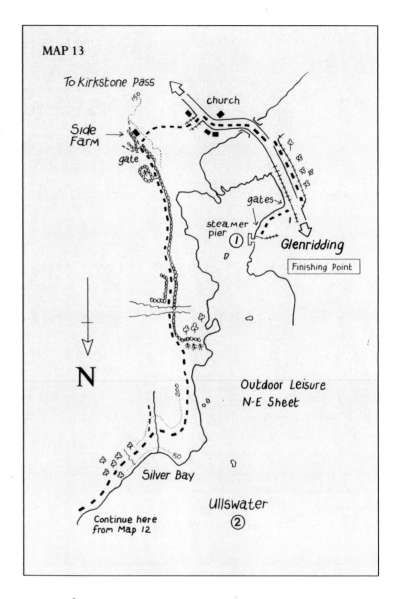

MAP 13

To Kirkstone Pass

church

Side Farm

gate

gates

steamer pier ①

Glenridding

Finishing Point

N

Outdoor Leisure N-E Sheet

Silver Bay

Continue here from Map 12

Ullswater ②

After ½ mile (0.8 km), the path descends to a kissing gate in a drystone wall (notice the log and chain closing mechanism on the gate). Twenty yards (18 m) farther on you pass through a gap in an old stone wall and the path leads you down onto open fields, leaving the trees behind you. The footpath goes straight across the field to a gate in a stone wall, whilst the shore line curves round to your R. As you walk across the field you will pass a signpost, indicating Howtown and Sandwick. Go across a second field to another gate and then bear L, across the third field, towards trees and another gate. This brings you into another field, alongside a stream. Follow the path and you cross a bridge and enter the tiny hamlet of Sandwick.

Turn L up the tarmac road for 100 yards (91 m) until you

pass the last of the attractive cottages on your R (the last one is Townend Cottage), then leave the road and turn R onto a grass track (PFS 'Patterdale'). The track goes steeply uphill for a few yards, then becomes level once more and follows the drystone wall on your right. You are now moving away from the lake shore and, as the wall becomes a fence, you have a view to fields sweeping down to the tree-lined shore. Ahead of you and to the R is Birk Fell.

Half a mile (0.8 km) along the wall you will pass a bank barn and come to a small beck. Cross and, where the path forks, bear half-R. The track descends to Scalehow Beck.

At this point you can make a worthwhile detour up the fellside on your L to an attractive, tree-lined waterfall.

Following the track once more, you go uphill again and eventually leave the stone wall behind and the view opens out. Across the lake you can see Gowbarrow Park (3). A mile (1.6 km) of rough, undulating track now winds above the shore, through trees and bracken, around to Silver Bay.

As you leave the trees, the track forks. Bear R, around the bay, and as you climb up past Silver Point you are greeted by a view of Glenridding. Follow the track and you will come to a ridge lined with tall conifers. After crossing two small becks, you start to walk between two stone walls until, after 200 yards (182 m), the enclosure on your L ends and you have open, bracken-covered fellside above you.

You begin a slow, gradual descent towards Side Farm (there is a campsite on the R). Disregard a couple of paths on your L as you approach the farm. Once you reach Side Farm, the first thing you will probably want to do is buy an ice cream. Thus provisioned, turn R through the farmyard and follow the track across fields to the main road.

Turn R and follow the road. This section of the walk is a little dull, but there is no way to avoid it (unless you bully a companion into fetching the car). After a $\frac{1}{4}$ mile (0.4 km), cross the road at a bridge and continue for the same distance again until you come to a small path on your L. Bear L, up the narrow path for about 600 yards (546 m) until it drops back to the road. Cross over and through a gate to follow the lake shore around a field. This brings you back into the car park at Glenridding pier.

1 The Ullswater launches

There are two launches which sail the lake from Glenridding to Pooley Bridge, both run by the grandly-named Ullswater Navigation and Transit Company Limited. *Lady of the Lake* was first launched in 1877 and her sister ship, *Raven*, in 1889. Originally steam-driven, today they are powered by diesel.

The Company runs a regular daily service from Easter to the end of October. (See Addresses, page 191.)

2 *Ullswater*

The lake is second only to Windermere in length but far surpasses it for peace and solitude. Although a navigable highway, there are few motor-driven vessels on the lake, the speed boats and water skiers having been driven away by the 10mph speed restriction imposed in 1983. At the northern end of the lake there is an underground pumping station which draws off water to feed the reservoir at Haweswater.

3 *Gowbarrow Park*

It was on April 15, 1802, whilst walking through Gowbarrow Woo[1] to visit their friends the Clarksons, at Eusemere, that William and Dorothy Wordsworth came upon a bank of daffodils. Later, Dorothy noted in her Journal: 'I never saw daffodils so beautiful, they grew among the mossy stones about and about them, some resting their heads upon these stones as on a pillow for weariness and the rest tossed and reeled and danced and seemed as if they verily laughed with the wind that blew upon them over the lake, they looked so gay ever glancing ever changing.' Two years later, William used Dorothy's observations as the basis of a poem and the 'host of golden daffodils' passed into the realm of literature.

Gowbarrow Park is now owned by the National Trust. The castellated tower you can glimpse above the tree tops is Lyulph's Tower, originally a hunting lodge built in the early 1800s by the Duke of Norfolk. The name—and that of the lake itself—is thought to derive from an early Norse settler, the first Lord of Ullswater.

Herdwick sheep near Sandwick

2·12

THE LANGDALE PIKES

STARTING AND FINISHING
POINT
Car park opposite the New Dungeon
Ghyll Hotel in Great Langdale
(SW-295064).
LENGTH
4 miles (6.4 km)
ASCENT
2440 feet (740 m)

It had to be done; no book of this nature could possibly ignore the traverse of the Langdale Pikes. Known locally as 'the tourist motorway', parts of this route have been subjected to so much erosion and subsequent footpath maintenance that they resemble a paved garden footpath. But only the ascent seems in the least artificial. Once beyond Stickle Tarn, you have a broad, open fell and an easy stroll between two of the best loved—and most easily recognized—peaks in Lakeland.

ROUTE DESCRIPTION (Map 14)

Leave the car park and cross the road to walk back towards the New Dungeon Ghyll Hotel. The little lane leads you past Stickle Barn, on your L, and the hotel proper on your R, and brings you to a small, white cottage. The route goes to the R of the cottage, through a wooden gate and into a field. Bear half-L across the field to a gap in the stone wall. Once through, continue between two wire fences for a few yards and then bear half-R (National Trust sign: 'Stickle Ghyll'). A rough, stone-covered track goes uphill, running alongside the beck. The path is heavily maintained from this point on.

You are climbing a rough, pasture field. After 50 yards (45 m), there is a nice waterfall on your R. Stickle Ghyll is a fast-flowing beck, carving a dramatic path through the rocks (it is interesting to speculate that what the Ghyll has taken thousands of years to achieve, fellwalkers look like matching in a few generations).

After 250 yards (227 m), cross the beck via a wooden footbridge and continue uphill, following the stream. Shortly, you will come to a wooden fence across the path. As you cross via the stile, look down at the little 'dog gate', thoughtfully provided alongside. Once over the fence, you come almost immediately to a major path joining you from the R. Bear L and continue uphill, crossing a small beck feeding Stickle Ghyll. Once across the stone footbridge, the path enters a stone wall sheep enclosure. Bear half-R, out of the sheep enclosure and

87

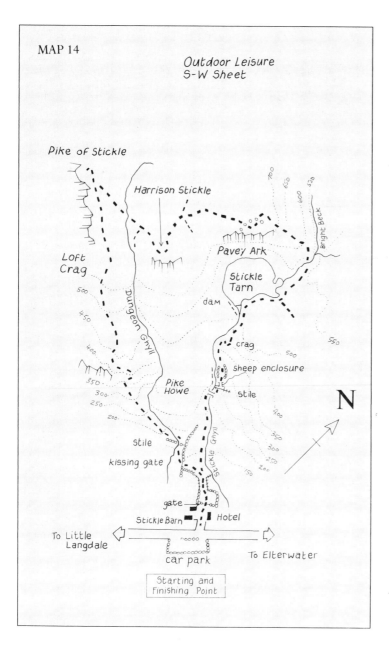

MAP 14

Outdoor Leisure
S-W Sheet

Pike of Stickle

Harrison Stickle

Loft
Crag

Pavey Ark

Stickle
Tarn

Bright Beck

dam

Dungeon Ghyll

crag

sheep enclosure

Pike
Howe

stile

N

Stickle Ghyll

stile

kissing gate

gate

Stickle Barn   Hotel

To Little
Langdale

To Elterwater

car park

Starting and
Finishing Point

begin to climb a short series of steps.

Consulting the OS map at this point may lead doubters to think that they are on the wrong side of the beck; footpath maintenance on this part of the fell has been so extensive that the L-hand bank is simply too loose and rough to be worth following. As on Cat Bells and other routes, the diversion signs should always be followed. Even so, the path becomes more eroded the higher you climb, though eventually this too will be

Sunrise viewed from the Langdale Pikes

paved and neat. Once above the steps, the path climbs quite steeply and begins to zigzag until you arrive at a steep crag with steps hacked into the rock. The path continues to zigzag up the side of the crag—a fairly easy, straightforward route, though in wet weather it can be boggy at the top of the crag. Once you've attained the summit of the crag, turn L and carry on upstream for a further 200 yards (182 m) until you arrive at Stickle Tarn.

An attractive tarn, 400 yards (364 m) across at its widest point, Stickle Tarn is overshadowed by the impressive crag which stands behind it—Pavey Ark. This is a good crag for rock climbers.

Follow the easy, level path to the R of the tarn. After 100 yards (91 m), there is a path peeling off to the R. Ignore this and carry straight on until you start to follow Bright Beck. Three hundred yards (273 m) from the tarn, the path crosses the beck and bears half-L to the northern ridge of Pavey Ark. There is a short, steep climb up the ridge to the top of the crag. It is rough underfoot in places, but quite easy to spot and the path is marked by occasional piles of stones. At the summit, bear L and cross a stone wall to stand at the top of the crag, giving you a dramatic view down to the tarn. Come off the rocks again and rejoin the main path.

Go L along the path, following it towards Harrison Stickle. It is easy to go wrong as you approach Harrison Stickle—there is a path which forks L to take you down the screes to Stickle Tarn. The junction comes shortly before two small tarns (which practically dry up during a warm summer). Continue following the stones along the main path, walking across the edge of a flat, moorland plateau. An easy climb to the top of Harrison follows. Walk out along the rocky peninsula and you have superb views of Bowfell, Crinkle Crags and Elterwater. It is easy to see why the Langdale 'traverse' has become so popular—it is a very quick route to attain the feeling of being among the mountains.

From Harrison Stickle, head back towards the main path once more and look out for a path bearing half-L, winding across the plateau towards the distinctive cone of Pike of Stickle, $\frac{1}{2}$ mile (0.8 km) away.

The footpath crosses a beck—about equidistant between the two peaks—and then climbs slowly to the peak. The final few yards are a scramble up the side before you stand on the flat, rocky summit of Pike of Stickle. The views from here are most impressive; you can look right down into Langdale and follow the line of the fells, along Rosset Gill and across Bowfell and the Crinkles, as they encircle Great Langdale valley.

Descend from Pike of Stickle via the same scramble and as you meet the outgoing path, bear R—instead of straight on—

to follow the line of the ridge towards Loft Crag—heading south-east, if in any doubt. The descent down Thorn Crag—on the far side of Dungeon Ghyll—is a very eroded path; more popular perhaps because it is the more obviously dramatic route off the Langdales.

Loft Crag is a gentle descent with good views. Frustratingly, the path does not go to the summit of the crag, but a detour is recommended. The path is waymarked with piles of stones and very easy to follow. As you round the side of Loft Crag, the route becomes steeper and less kind on the calf muscles. Once down a stretch of scree, the path levels out once more across a sloping, grassy fellside. The hill to your R falls away very quickly as you walk across the top of White Crag. After a short distance, Dungeon Ghyll (the beck, not the hotel) comes into view on your L. There is a final steep descent—which gives a good view of the waterfall—and the route joins up with the beck.

You eventually cross the beck at a point where two stone walls meet, forming the corner of a field. Climb to the L-hand wall and cross via a stile. Once through, continue downhill with the beck on your R. The path follows the stone wall on your L for a short distance until you come alongside a farm gate and a kissing gate. Go through and go straight down to rejoin the outgoing path at the field behind the New Dungeon Ghyll Hotel.

Pavey Ark in mist from the slopes of Harrison Stickle

WANSFELL

STARTING AND FINISHING
POINT
Ambleside village centre. Use the
main car park, opposite Charlotte
Mason College, as your starting point
(SE-376047).
LENGTH
6 miles (9.6 km)
ASCENT
1700 ft (515 m)

It is easy to dismiss Wansfell as a quick trot up the fellside
before tea time. Don't be misled; it is steep—in fact, it's very
steep—but the superb view across the head of Lake Windermere makes it all worthwhile. A gentle descent and a stroll
through the historic village of Troutbeck are followed by a
pleasant walk along Robin Lane and Skelghyll Wood and back
into Ambleside.

ROUTE DESCRIPTION (Map 15)

Leave the car park via the narrow footbridge which crosses
Stock Ghyll and turn R along the road *(1)*. Follow the traffic
back into the village, past the market cross and the ugly new
pedestrian crossing, until you come to the Salutation Hotel.
Turn L, along a short lane, until you come to a sign which says,
simply, 'The Waterfalls'. Turn L and follow the lane round the
back of the Salutation, walking uphill until you come to a broad
track on your L, signed Stock Ghyll Park and Waterfalls. Turn L
here and walk into the trees, following the path alongside the
beck, past an old sluice gate to a footbridge. Cross the beck and
continue uphill, following the path to the waterfalls *(2)*.

  Above the falls, cross the stone bridge and bear L, away from
the falls. The path takes you back to the lane. Go through the
strange, turnstile gate and turn L along the lane, heading uphill
once more.

  About ½ mile (0.8 km) from the village, you will come to a
farm gate across your path (signed: Grove Farm). Go through
and continue along the tarmac track for another 150 yards
(136 m) until you pass a ladder stile in the stone wall on your R
(PFS 'Troutbeck via Wansfell'). Climb over the stile and you are
in a steep, fellside field. Go straight uphill, following a tiny beck
on your L.

  You climb very quickly and have a good view back over the
village to Loughrigg Fell and the Langdales. After 400 yards
(364 m) of stiff ascent, the footpath crosses over the beck and
continues uphill to meet an old stone wall which comes in from

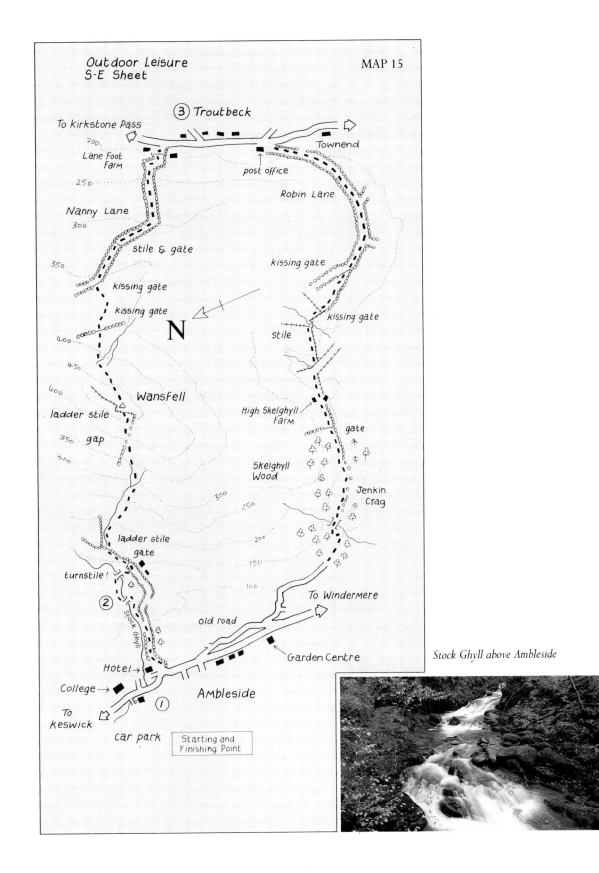

Outdoor Leisure
S-E Sheet

MAP 15

③ Troutbeck

To kirkstone Pass

Townend

200

Lane Foot
Farm

post office

250

Robin Lane

Nanny Lane

300

stile & gate

kissing gate

350

kissing gate

stile

kissing gate

kissing gate

400

N

450

400

Wansfell

ladder stile

350   gap

High Skelghyll
Farm

gate

300

Skelghyll
Wood

300

250

Jenkin
Crag

ladder stile

gate

200

turnstile!

150

②

Stock Ghyll

100

To Windermere

old road

Hotel →

Garden Centre

College →

Ambleside

To
Keswick

①

car park

Starting and
Finishing Point

Stock Ghyll above Ambleside

your L. Follow the wall for a few yards and then go through a gap and up to a ladder stile. Once across there is a short pull to the summit of Wansfell.

This is a superb viewpoint with grand views down the length of Lake Windermere. From the summit, follow the line of cairns down to the east, through a gate and past a turning to your R (PFS 'Troutbeck via the Hundred Road'). Do not turn, but continue straight ahead until you come to another wall. Go through the kissing gate and turn R down a rough track which runs between two stone walls. This part of the route is known as Nanny Lane and it brings you, after almost $\frac{3}{4}$ mile (1.2 km) of steady walking, down to Troutbeck village. During the descent you get a wonderful view across the valley to High Street and Ill Bell.

The track passes through Lane Foot Farm and you emerge onto the main road. Turn R and follow the road through Troutbeck village *(3)*. After $\frac{1}{2}$ mile (0.8 km) you will come to the post office on your right and a track which bears off the road (PBS Ambleside). Turn R up this track (which is known as Robin Lane) and follow it uphill, around the southern flank of Wansfell.

Keep to the track for $\frac{3}{4}$ mile (1.2 km) (disregarding two paths off to your L en route) until you pass a kissing gate in the wall to your L, marked 'Skelghyll and Ambleside'. Turn L through the gate and follow a path across a field, downhill. You pass through another kissing gate and cross a beck. Follow the wire fence on your L and this will bring you down to a tarmac track leading to High Skelghyll Farm. Turn R, cross the cattle grid, and follow the track towards the farm.

The track leads you through the farmyard and onto a rougher track which winds across the fellside and gives you good views down the lake to Belle Isle *(4)*. Two hundred yards (182 m) beyond the farm, the track goes through a gate into Skelghyll Wood. Follow an easy route through mixed woodland and after a $\frac{1}{4}$ mile (0.4 km) begin to look out for a sign to Jenkin Crag, on your L. This is a fine viewpoint, enabling you to look across the head of the lake to the Langdales and the fells of central Lakeland.

Return to the path and continue downhill, crossing the beck via a pretty stone bridge. Continue down through the trees and the path bears away from the beck to join a tarmac lane. Follow the lane downhill and you emerge on the old Ambleside road, above the A591, at a point just opposite Hayes garden centre. Turn R and follow the old road back into Ambleside.

Lake Windermere from Wansfell

1 The Bridge House

As you walk towards the village centre you cannot fail to notice one of the Lake District's most famous buildings on your right, the Bridge House. This is now a National Trust information centre and shop. It stands right over Stock Ghyll, leading to the legend that it was originally built by a wily Scotsman to evade Land Tax. The truth, however, is more prosaic; it began life as an apple store for Ambleside Hall, when this part of the village consisted of orchard. In its time it has also served as a weaver's shop, a family home, a cobbler's and a tea shop.

2 Stockghyll Force

Very popular with the Victorians, Stockghyll Force is a 90 foot (27 m) cascade hidden in the trees above Ambleside. At one stage, as at Lodore in Borrowdale, a turnstile was installed and a charge of 3 old pence was made to see the falls. The ghyll has also had its industrial uses—witness the sluice gate as you enter the park. At one time it provided power for up to three local fulling mills; the waterwheel of one of these mills is still visible a little lower down the beck, in the village.

3 Troutbeck

Troutbeck is a string of hamlets, each centred about a communal well, most of them named after saints. You will pass two of these wells on your right as you walk along the road. The buildings date mostly from the seventeenth and eighteenth centuries. The best of them is Townend, a former statesman-farmer's house, built around 1626. It is more elaborate than a normal farmer's house of the period and contains some fine furniture and oak panelling. It is owned by the National Trust and is undoubtedly their finest house open to the public in the Lake District.

4 Belle Isle

This island is the only one on Windermere to be inhabited. At 38 acres (15 hectares), it is also the largest island on the lake and it contains an unusual and elegant round house, said to be the only completely round house in England. It was built in 1774 and passed into the hands of Isabella Curwen, after whom the island—formerly Long Holm—was renamed. It remains in the Curwen family to this day and is open to the public during the summer. Access is via special launch from Bowness Bay.

BLENCATHRA

A tiny car park along the minor road, just past the White Horse Inn (NE-348273), near Scales on the A66 (Penrith–Cockermouth road)
LENGTH
5½ miles (8.8 km)
ASCENT
2180 ft (660 m)

Sometimes called Saddleback—a sad example of dereliction of the English language—Blencathra lacks Skiddaw's popularity but has more character. This walk is straightforward until you ascend Sharp Edge. This is a prominent arête which towers over Scales Tarn and can leave you feeling exposed and vulnerable. Consult your nerves before setting out (and be honest).

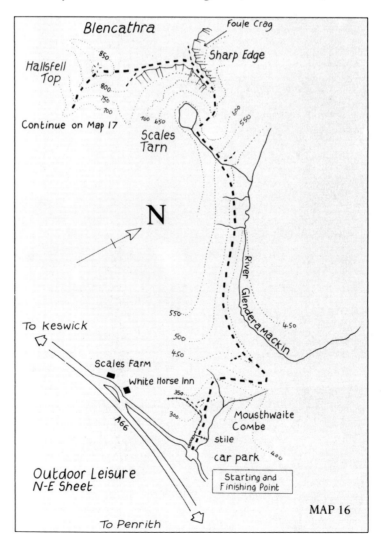

MAP 16

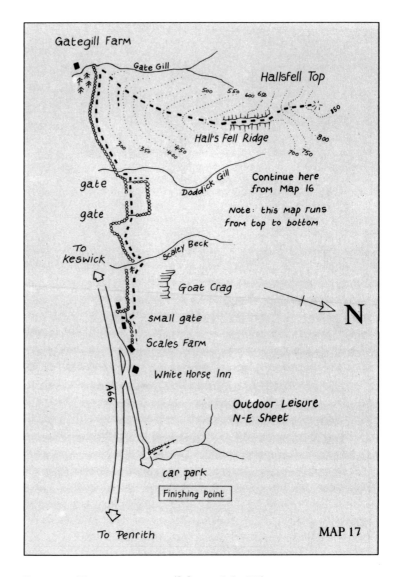

Gategill Farm

Gate Gill

Hallsfell Top

500 550 600 650

150

Hall's Fell Ridge

800

300 350 400 450

700 750

gate

Doddick Gill

Continue here
from Map 16

gate

Note: this map runs
from top to bottom

To
Keswick

Scaley Beck

Goat Crag

N

small gate

Scales Farm

White Horse Inn

A66

Outdoor Leisure
N-E Sheet

car park

Finishing Point

MAP 17

To Penrith

ROUTE DESCRIPTION (Maps 16, 17)

Walk back along the road, over the stone bridge and look out
for a slate sign in a wall on your R: 'Glenderamackin 1,
Mungrisedale 3'. At this point, turn R, along a track to a farm
gate. Cross via the stile alongside and keep straight ahead,
following the wire fence on your L. Walk along the edge of a
marshy field and the fence becomes a low, hawthorn hedge.
Ahead you can see the footpath winding up a broad, green ridge.
After 100 yards (91 m), the footpath starts to follow the field
boundary around to the left. Stay with it for 10 yards (9 m) until
you come to a gate on your L; the footpath bears off to the R at
this point. Keep following the path which is quite clear as it
strikes out towards the fellside. A fold in the hills turns

The ascent of Sharp Edge

Mousthwaite Comb into a gigantic bowl, open towards the A66, and you are walking around the base of this bowl. The footpath bears R again and begins to ascend the grassy flanks of the ridge between Souther Fell and Scales Fell.

Once at the top of the ridge, turn L towards Scales Fell and you have a good view of Sharp Edge on Blencathra. Follow the ridge and after 400 yards (364 m) you will be joined by a footpath coming in from your L. Below you is an excellent view of River Glenderamackin and the wide, grassy track which runs along the far bank up to the old lead mines.

You follow a fairly eroded path, climbing gradually until you meet up with Scales Beck. Turn L and follow the path uphill, crossing the beck so that the water runs on your L. The path is quite steep and runs through a small gully. After 300 yards (273 m) you climb the rise to arrive at Scales Tarn.

This is a peaceful little tarn, dramatically placed against Tarn Crags and Sharp Edge. The tarn itself is quite shallow and you can see the bottom as it gently shelves away. Sharp Edge is the magnificent arête on your R. It is best to try and arrive at this point fairly early in the day to get up onto the ridge.

Climb the steep path running up to the start of the ridge and then begin to walk out onto the rocks. There are steep drops on either side of you. At the beginning, there is a path which runs 5 feet (1.5 m) below the top of the ridge, on the R—though you still get purists who insist on walking along the absolute apex.

The route can be a scramble in some places. The final stretch of the ridge involves walking past a boulder which seems to lean out over the path; in fact, there is plenty of room to simply walk past and you will only have difficulties if you start to hug too close to the rock. As you reach the end of Sharp Edge you are confronted by the aptly-named Foule Crag. This is a steep, rough scramble before you find yourself on a steeply rolling grass slope and climb to the summit of Blencathra.

Once at the top, all is peace and tranquility after the excitement and tensions of the ascent. Before you is a broad, open moorland plateau. Follow the path as it curves gently round to the summit cairn.

The views from here can be absolutely exhilarating. Look below to Threlkeld and follow the line of the river eastwards until you come to an old railway viaduct *(1)*.

As you face south, the footpath off the summit lies directly in front of you and starts with another steep drop. You come down onto a clearly defined footpath which proceeds down Hall's Fell Ridge. This rocky ridge is quite easy to negotiate, taking a certain amount of care across any loose stone and rubble but can be treacherous in wet or icy conditions. Doddick Gill forms a steep gorge to your L. After just over $\frac{1}{2}$ mile (0.8 km), you start to level off across a heather-covered fellside. Continue down to Gategill Farm, ignoring the path on your L as you get within 200 yards (182 m) of the farm. You approach a stone wall, enclosing a conifer plantation, just behind the farm. Turn L and follow the wall along the foot of the fellside.

The path crosses Doddick Gill and continues along the wall until, almost 1 mile (1.6 km) from Gate Gill, it drops down a shallow gorge to cross Scaley Beck. Once across onto the other bank, resume following the wall until you come to a kissing gate on your R. Go through, between two cottages, and you find yourself beside the A66. Turn L, following the road past Scales Farm to the White Horse Inn, whereupon you bear L onto the minor road which takes you back to the car.

1 Mosedale Viaduct

This was once part of the line that connected Penrith and Cockermouth. When the line opened, in 1865, it put Keswick on the Victorian tourist map. The route eventually fell foul of Beeching's axe, but the section from Threlkeld to Keswick has recently been re-opened as a delightful, low-level footpath. A walk sheet giving map and directions is available from any National Park information centre.

Looking down on Scales Tarn from Foule Crag

2·15

GLARAMARA

STARTING AND FINISHING
POINT
NPA car park in Seatoller, Borrowdale
(NW-246138).
LENGTH
8 miles (12.8 km)
ASCENT
2340 ft (708 m)

The majority who walk the slopes of Glaramara invariably do so en route to other mountains, merely using the fell as a stepping stone to higher and greater things. This is a pity as it can form the basis for an energetic afternoon ramble.

ROUTE DESCRIPTION (Maps 18, 19)

Leaving Seatoller, head back along the road towards Rosthwaite until you cross Strands Bridge. Turn R (just opposite a terrace of white-fronted houses, marked 'Mountain View' on the OS map) and walk down a narrow lane, following a sign for Thorney-thwaite Farm. After 100 yards (91 m), you will pass a ladder stile on your L. Ignoring this, continue to a farm gate (signed: 'Public Footpath') and turn L. Follow the grassy track as it crosses a rough, fellside field.

The track swings round to the R to climb alongside a drystone wall. Behind the wall you can hear the tantalizing sound of running water and as you pass beyond the end of the wall Combe Gill can be seen, a short distance below you. You climb up to a kissing gate and once through, the path can be clearly seen, winding across the hillside ahead.

As you follow the path across the side of Thorneythwaite Fell, you are able to look along the valley to the dark, curving crag at the head of Combe Gill *(1)*. Two hundred yards (182 m) from the kissing gate, there is a footpath which bears L and follows the gill to the head of the valley, and a steep climb to Combe Door. This can be an impressive alternative route—albeit very hard work—but can be very damp and boggy at the valley head after a wet spell.

Disregarding the L-hand path, carry straight on, following an eroded streak across the fellside. Five hundred yards (455 m) beyond the fork in the path, the route becomes a little indistinct; veer slightly to your R, to climb steeply alongside a narrow gully. The path becomes rough and clear once more, swinging L and bringing you up onto the ridge of the fell. As you climb above the valley floor, you should take the opportunity to

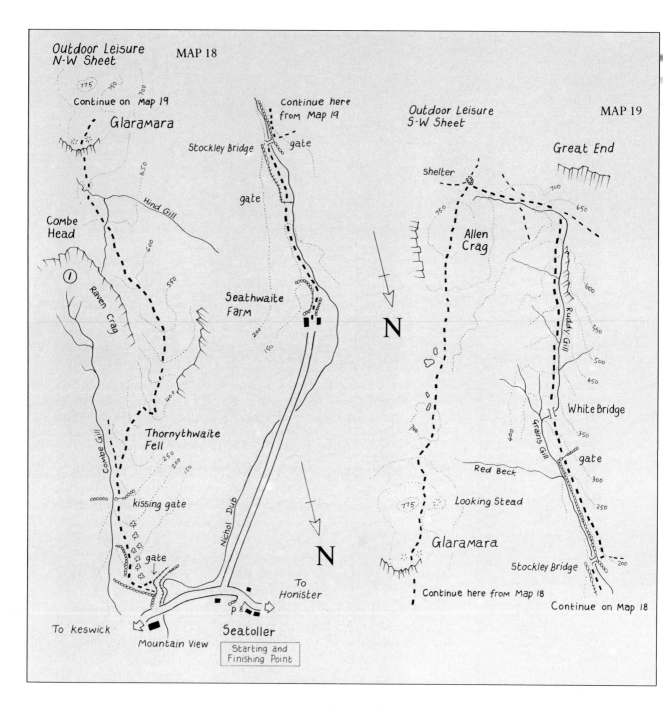

Map 18 / Map 19 (hand-drawn walking route map)

Opposite~Langdale Pikes from the summit of Glaramara. Pike of Stickle is the distinctive cone in the distance.

turn round now and again for a superb view through the Jaws of Borrowdale to Derwent Water and Keswick. This gets better the higher that you climb.

You arrive on a boggy plateau above Raven Crag, with a good view to Sourmilk Gill on your R. The path becomes a little indistinct again here; you should be heading towards a rock outcrop and a solitary ash tree. Bear round to the R of the

outcrop and continue uphill towards a craggy knoll ahead of you—Combe Head.

The path leaves Combe Head on your L and crosses a pair of narrow becks—the source of Hind Gill, which plunges over the crags to Seathwaite, on your R. A final pull across the fell and you arrive at the foot of a dark crag. A very easy rock climb of perhaps 20 feet (6 m) lies between you and the summit of Glaramara. Once at the top of the rock face, the summit is the cairn on your R; the north eastern of the two little peaks.

Follow the path across the tops, heading roughly southwards and following an easy route across a grassy moorland. After a while, the path starts to go downhill and drops to a small, boggy col before climbing once more across the rocks to Allen Crags, passing a number of small tarns en route. An excellent view of Great End lies to your R. Allen Crag is a little, rocky summit, looking down over Angle Tarn and Esk Hause. Drop down the other side of the crag to a major junction of paths at a large stone shelter.

This is a fairly bleak spot, a meeting of mountains. At the shelter, turn R, to head north-west, and follow the path down to the broad bend of Ruddy Gill.

After nearly $\frac{1}{2}$ mile (0.8 km), as you come level with the crag of Great End on the L, the river plunges away to the R, down a steep and attractive gorge. Cross the river and follow the path downstream. After perhaps $\frac{1}{2}$ mile (0.8 km) of steady, downhill walking, you will come to a wooden bridge. Cross over and continue downhill, with Grains Gill on your R. This part of the path has been heavily maintained and brings you to a gate in a stone wall which lies across your route. Go through and carry on downhill. You pick up a wall on your R which you should follow until you arrive at a split in the path. Turn R and immediately through a farm gate and over Stockley Bridge.

The path takes you downhill, through another gate, and onto the valley floor. Follow the rough path towards a group of farm buildings ahead of you. This brings you to Seathwaite Farm. Go through the farmyard and onto the tarmac lane beyond. Follow the lane to the junction with the main Borrowdale road. Turn L and follow the road back to Seatoller.

1 Combe Gill (or Comb Gill, on older maps)
Combe Gill, a gigantic hollow, scooped out from the mountain wall is an excellent example of a hanging valley—perhaps for this reason, school parties can frequently be seen plodding across the boggy valley floor. At the valley head is the biggest natural cave in the Lake District—but take heed of any warning notices advising you to keep away.

2·16

GREAT GABLE

STARTING AND FINISHING
POINT
Car park at Honister Hause
(NW-225136).
LENGTH
5¾ miles (9.2 km)
ASCENT
2200 ft (666 m)

Although the summit of Great Gable is rather flat and boring, being little more than a boulder field, the approach march around Brandreth is superb and the views from the summit are exhilarating. The starting point, at Honister Hause, gains you over 1100 feet (335 m) before you even leave the car, making this a splendid long afternoon walk.

ROUTE DESCRIPTION (Map 20)

At the end of the car park, next to the slate works, there is a farm gate and alongside a short flight of stone steps (PBS 'Great Gable, Dubs'). Cross the stile at the top of the steps and, after 5 yards (4.5 m) cross another stile to emerge onto the roadside. Turn L and follow the road for 40 yards (36 m) until you come to a green iron gate at the entrance to the slate works *(1)*. Go through the small, wooden gate alongside (signed: Public Bridleway) and bear R, past the buildings. Shortly beyond the buildings there is a sign on your L—'Danger quarry road, advised alternative route'—and the track forks. Go L, up a steep slate track.

As you climb, look right across the valley to Dalehead and the Yew Crag Quarries (now disused). If you look carefully you will be able to see a stretch of railway track coming straight down the fellside.

After climbing 400 feet (120 m), the track begins to level off across grass-covered fellside and climbs to a dismantled tramway. Carry straight on, over the first of the old sleepers lying across the path and up onto the embanked section. After 20 yards (18 m) you will see an obvious path on your L, marked by a line of small cairns. Turn L onto this path and follow it across open moorland. The cairns are at very regular intervals and after ¼ mile (0.4 km) you begin to have good views down to Buttermere and Crummock Water. The path ascends steadily at a gentle gradient but becomes very rough underfoot.

As you approach the ridge, almost 1 mile (1.6 km) from the tramway, a number of minor paths begin to split off. Keep to the main path and you come to the remnants of a boundary fence – now marked only by a line of rusty fence posts. At the fence, turn R and follow the line of posts downhill for 120 yards (109 m) until you come to a strong path cutting across the line of the fence in front of you. Turn L and follow the path, marked by lines of stones. The footpath becomes broad and eroded as you follow it over the ridge.

You are now walking at the very head of Ennerdale. Ahead of you are Great Gable and Kirk Fell (the latter with its very distinctive flat summit) and if you look to your R and behind a little, you can see the forest of Ennerdale and Black Sail Youth Hostel *(2)*.

You are walking down a broad, rounded fellside until you come to Stone Cove, directly beneath Windy Gap. This area is well-named and is a riot of boulders and scree. You pass a large cairn on your left and 20 yards (18 m) beyond that come to a small gill. A path goes L, along the gill to Windy Gap. Do not follow this but keep straight on to cross the beck and follow a very obvious path across the boulder field. The sombre bulk of Gable Crag looms above you on your L as you pick your way across the boulders and climb up to Beck Head.

This is a rocky, level area with good views down Ennerdale and back along the route you have just followed. You have a tremendous feeling of isolation here with mountain peaks stretching away into the distance on all sides.

As you attain the plateau there is a steep path running up the ridge of Great Gable, on your L. Although not the OS right-of-way, this route is easy to follow (by eye if not by foot, being very steep and rugged). Across the boulders there is a line of tiny cairns to mark the way up. After a final scramble to the top, you are greeted by a boulder field and a short walk to the summit cairn *(3)*.

Although the actual summit of Great Gable is not a great deal to boast about, it commands some of the finest views of any peak in the Lake District. The landscape is dominated by mountains. A short walk to the south of the main cairn and you will encounter another large cairn, known as the Westmorland Cairn *(4)*.

Walk away from the summit cairn in a north-easterly direction and you will pick up a line of stones to mark the route off Great Gable and down to Windy Gap. As you drop over the side the path becomes very steep and rocky. As you descend, Styhead Tarn comes into view (invariably surrounded by tents during the Duke of Edinburgh Award season). Once down at

View of Great Gable from Westmorland Cairn on Wasdale Head

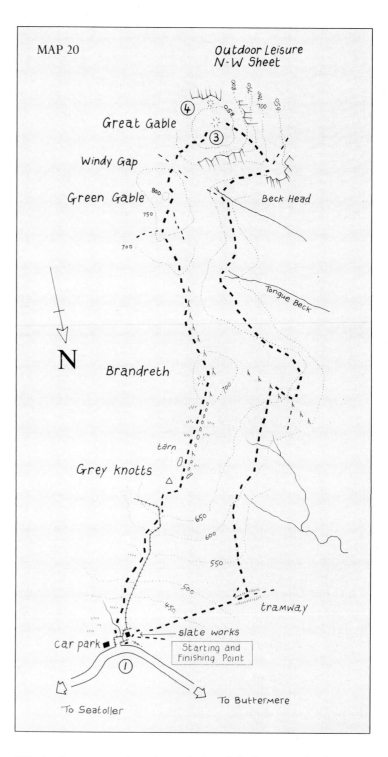

MAP 20

Outdoor Leisure
N-W Sheet

Windy Gap, a very broad, eroded path before you leads to the summit of Green Gable.

Mercifully, this ascent is quite short. Green Gable lives up to its name, a grassy, rounded fell, in marked contrast to Great

Gable which is almost devoid of vegetation. A clear footpath leads off the summit, marked by cairns. After 200 yards, (182 m) the path forks. Bear half-L across a flat, open fellside, following the cairns towards Brandreth. You pick up another line of fence posts and, as you approach the summit of Brandreth, the stones peel off to the L. Keep to the fence posts until you reach the rocky summit. From Brandreth, head north-east again, towards Grey Knotts and a straight, eroded path in front of you. The path is marked by piles of stones once more and you begin to run along another line of fence posts. Walk past a number of small tarns and the path takes you amongst rock outcrops at the summit of Grey Knotts.

The fence line turns sharply R, around an outcrop topped by a cairn. The path at this point is indistinct, so keep with the fence and follow it steeply downhill until you meet a wire fence in front of you, coming up from the valley. Go to the L of the new fence and you will come to a wooden stile. Cross the fence and continue downhill with the wire fence on your L.

You should keep to the fence at all times and follow a steep descent across a grassy fellside, back towards the slate works. The path is muddy in places, but otherwise easy to follow and you soon come within sight of the car park. Follow the path down through the yard at the back of the works, cross the quarry road and through a small wooden gate to re-enter the car park.

1 *Honister Quarry*

The quarries at Honister have been producing the distinctive green slate (in great demand as a high grade building material) for over 300 years. At one time, the blocks of stone were brought down the fell on wooden sleds until the tram ways came into use towards the end of the nineteenth century. Today, the stone is carried down by lorry, but the final 'dressing' of the slate—working it into the required shape— is still largely accomplished by hand. In recent years the Buttermere and Westmorland Green Slate Company Ltd has enjoyed a boom in business, with export orders from all over the globe.

2 *Ennerdale*

Ennerdale is the only one of the sixteen lakes to lack a metalled road travelling its length. Probably because of this, the valley remains a quiet, peaceful place where it is easy to get away from the crowds of central Lakeland. Cars are only permitted as far as Bowness Knott, at the western tip of the lake—thereafter the valley is the exclusive preserve of the walker.

Looking back at Great Gable from Brandreth, on the return route

The valley was heavily afforested during the 1930s, causing an uproar of protest which forced the Forestry Commission to take a more sympathetic approach to seeding the fells. In recent years, they have also opened up the head of the valley to walkers, with the Nine Becks Walk and the Smithy Beck Trail. Walk leaflets are available at Bowness Knott car park.

At the head of the valley stands Black Sail Youth Hostel. Completely inaccessible by car, it is little more than a mountain hut, with a total of eighteen beds.

3 *Summit Cairn*

On the north side of the summit cairn there is a bronze plaque which bears a relief map of the summit and the following inscription:

'The Fell and Rock Climbing Club.
In glorious and happy memory of those whose names are inscribed below, members of this club who died for their country in the European War, 1914–1918. These fells were acquired by their fellow members and by them vested in the National Trust for the use and enjoyment of the people of our land for all time.'

The club purchased just over a thousand acres—shown on the plaque—in 1923 and the memorial was unveiled the following year. The Fell and Rock Climbing Club continues to hold a commemorative service every year on this spot, on Remembrance Sunday.

4 *The Westmorland Cairn*

Just south of the summit there stands a large stone cairn, built in the 1870s by Edward and Thomas Westmorland. It marks what they felt to be the finest view in the Lake District. As you stand here, looking down over Wasdale, it is hard to disagree.

DERWENT WATER

STARTING AND FINISHING POINT
Car park near to the Century Theatre on Lake Road, Keswick (NW-265230).
LENGTH
10 miles (16 km)
ASCENT
165 ft (50 m)

Derwent Water has been called the Queen of the Lakes. Its beauty undoubtedly comes from its setting, flanked by mountains at the entrance to the Borrowdale Valley. It is possible to make a complete circuit of the lake on foot, but one of the particular joys of this route is that you are shadowed by the lake launches all the way. If you tire of walking, simply catch a boat at the next landing stage.

ROUTE DESCRIPTION (Maps 21, 22)

Walk down the road to the landing stages. This is the beginning of the walk. If you are not feeling terribly energetic, take the launch to Lodore. This way you will miss one or two nice promontories and lakeside meadows, but you will also avoid a tedious scramble and roadside section. However, if you are a purist, and only a complete circuit will do, follow the metalled road southwards, past the NT shop to a gravelled pathway, signed: 'National Trust—Friar's Crag'. Follow the path until it brings you to a stone memorial to John Ruskin *(1)*. A little farther on you will come to a superb promontory (Friar's Crag) and a view across the water to Derwent Island. *(2)*.

Turning back from the view, follow the path round to the R, going through a gate and bearing round the lake shore. This takes you across a beck before once more diving into the trees via another small gate. You catch a glimpse to your left of Skiddaw and the tapering spire of St John's Church in the foreground.

The woodland path bears away from the shore, crossing a beck via a flat wooden bridge, before making a dog-leg at a fine hedge. Follow the hedgerow and then a ditch until you come to a farm gate. Go through the small gate alongside and climb the bank to the road. Turn R along the road.

The road leads you past the pristine grounds of Stable Hill. Look out for another farm gate on your R, which takes you into a field. The path heads towards the shore again. Follow the path to a small gate and through another wooded promontory—

Lake launch at Lodore landing

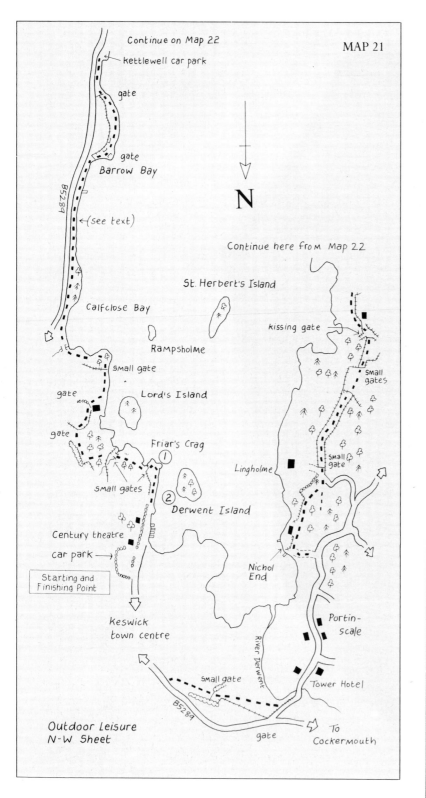

Calfclose Bay, Derwent Water

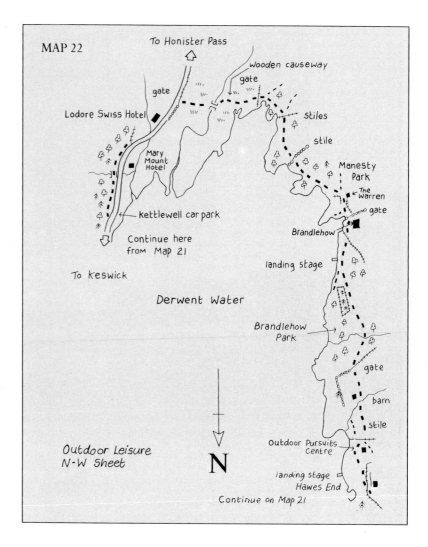

MAP 22

To Honister Pass

Wooden causeway

gate

gate

Lodore Swiss Hotel

stiles

stile

Mary Mount Hotel

Manesty Park

The Warren

gate

Brandlehow

Kettlewell car park

landing stage

Continue here from Map 21

To Keswick

Derwent Water

Brandlehow Park

gate

barn

stile

Outdoor Pursuits Centre

Outdoor Leisure N-W Sheet

N

landing stage Hawes End

Continue on Map 21

every bit as nice as Friar's Crag but infinitely more peaceful.

The path brings you back towards the road and from this point onwards, flirts with the main road, approaching it and then bearing away again. As the space between the shoreline and the road lessens, you may find it necessary to walk along the road if the lake is high after heavy rainfall. This can be a risky business, even at quiet times of the year.

At Barrow Bay, you can sample another bit of lakeshore, going through a gate, over a little bridge and crossing a narrow, grassy field. The gate at the far end leads back to the road. You are now at Kettlewell car park. If you do not fancy more road work, cross over into the wood on the opposite side and turn R, following a rough path past Mary Mount Hotel until you come back to the road, just by a field boundary, within sight of the Lodore Swiss Hotel. Cross the road and continue past the hotel; after 500 yards (455 m) you will come to a farm gate on your R.

Turn R, through the gate (PFS 'Manesty'). A wide, gravelly track—liable to flooding in very wet weather—marches straight towards the reed beds at the head of the lake. A gated bridge of rather fine proportions carries you over the channel of the River Derwent and leads to a wooden causeway, complete with passing places. Two-thirds of the way across the marshy ground, there is a little rocky knoll and another section of causeway before you regain terra firma.

For the next section, work your way around the lakeshore, disregarding any tracks which lead away from the water. An open, wooded section of oaks and Scots pines to the R of the path leads to a seat on a rocky promontory. Good views from here to Shepherd's Crag and the Lodore. Farther along you will come to a pair of stiles in a wire fence. This is shortly followed by yet another stile as the pleasant path meanders along the shore. The well-marked track leads through Manesty Park, over numerous little water channels, before reaching a forest track at a cottage called 'The Warren'. Turn R along the track and you will come to a boathouse and jetty by a house called 'Brandlehow'. The route slips in front of the house, curving away from the lake to reach a junction with a footpath, leading down from the main road. Go through a gate and down a short series of stone steps towards a jetty. The path now forges ahead, crossing several other routes through Brandlehow Park.

At the edge of the wood, you come to a point at which a fence and a stone wall meet at a gate. Go through the gate and the grassy track leads downhill. Stay on the route you are following, past an old barn, until you reach a stile just before an Outdoor Pursuits Centre. Then work your way downhill to the lower track, which has been visible for some time. The right-of-way passes in front of Hawes End House by way of a stile and gate and a section of metalled drive. Take care to stay on the path; large notices warn you of forbidden routes.

At a turning circle, beyond the main entrance to the grounds, take the footpath signed: To Portinscale, through a kissing gate. The fenced path leads through a wooded section, down to a gated bridge across a little beck. By this route, a wide, tree-fringed field is reached and crossed, the gate on the opposite side of the field leading to another wooded section of path. The lake is hidden from view by the rounded contours of Stub Hill, and shortly afterwards the boundary of Lingholme Gardens, with its many fine trees and colourful azaleas, is reached. A little black gate beside the main entrance allows you to cross the road and continue via the broad woodland path opposite into Fawe Park. At the intersection, go R, past a couple of cottages to the boat yard and jetty at Nichol End. If you wish to shorten the

walk, you can catch a launch here back to Keswick.

Those stalwart enough to continue should swing L, away from the lakeshore and along the drive to the main road. Turn R and follow the road into Portinscale. After the garage, the road forks by the post office. Turn R and walk past the Tower Hotel to the impressive suspended walkway over the River Derwent.

A short distance along the old road on the Keswick side, a double iron gate leads to a fine, flat path through two meadows. Eventually, you must join the A591; however you are nearly at the town centre and a brief stroll past the shops will take you past the Moot Hall and down Lake Road to the car park.

1   *Friar's Crag and the Ruskin Memorial*
The stone memorial to Ruskin bears the inscription:
> 'The first thing which I remember
> As an event in my life was being
> taken by my nurse to the brow of
> Friar's Crag on Derwentwater.'

(For further details of Ruskin, see Route 26, The Old Man of Coniston.) Friar's Crag is so named because it is said to have been the embarkation point for monks making a pilgrimage to St Herbert's Island (see below).

2   *Derwent Island and beyond*
Known to eighteenth-century guide books as Pocklington's Island, after Joseph Pocklington, an eccentric bachelor who bought the island in 1778 (it was then called Vicar's Island). He built a house and a series of follies, including a Druid's temple and a stone circle (which fooled nobody; William Gell referred to them as 'an awkward jumble of fantastic gew gaws'). Derwent Island lies to the right. Out in the middle of the lake is St Herbert's Island, once the hermitage of St Herbert, the disciple and close friend of St Cuthbert (the two were so attached that they are supposed to have died on the same day in 678). Derwent Water has five islands in all; of the remaining three, Rampsholme and Lord's Island are normal enough, but the last, is a real oddity and only occasionally apparent. Sometimes marked on maps as Floating Island, it lurks down in the south-west corner of the lake. A mass of floating weed and vegetation, kept buoyant by marsh gases, it only makes an appearance about once every three years or so.

Lake launch on Derwent Water

Sergeant Man

STARTING AND FINISHING POINT
Car park in Easedale Road, just beyond Grasmere village centre (SE-334080)
LENGTH
8 miles (13 km)
ASCENT
2250 ft (682 m)

It was William Wordsworth who first described the Lake District as resembling a wheel, the lakes radiating out like spokes. If this is so, then when you are on top of Sergeant Man you are standing on the hub. This 2430 ft (726 m) summit is dwarfed by its loftier cousins to the west but has a charm of its own; mainly due to the wonderful, bird's eye view of Stickle Tarn and Pavey Ark.

This walk approaches Sergeant Man via Easedale Tarn—surely one of the most popular tarns in the Lake District?—and returns along Far Easedale, a delightful, peaceful valley.

ROUTE DESCRIPTION (Map 23)

Turn R from the car park, rejoining Easedale Road and walking away from Grasmere village centre. The road passes over Goody Bridge and, 100 yards (91 m) on, passes a turning to the R. Keep straight on. This is a very pleasant little lane but at weekends it can become quite crowded with fellwalkers, all of them determined to do the same route that you are doing. 500 yards (455 m) from the car park, the road bends round to the R. In front of you is a small wood, which you enter via a stone bridge over Easedale Beck (NT sign: 'Easedale'). Continue straight ahead, through the trees and crossing a smaller beck. Once over this last beck, you are on a wide track which leads to a farm gate. The broad, stoney track continues alongside the beck, on your R, leading across the fields. Directly ahead of you, in the distance, you can see Sourmilk Gill, and the low, rolling fellside to your L is Silver How.

After 200 yards (182 m) the path is joined by a stone wall on the left. After a further 250 yards (227 m), you pass a farm gate on your L signed: Blind Moss Tarn. Shortly after, the wall becomes a wire fence and you come to a farm gate across the path. Once through, you find yourself in an open field, the path bearing half-L across a concrete bridge, leaving the beck away to your R. The beck makes a big loop and rejoins the footpath as you approach another farm gate in front of you. This takes you

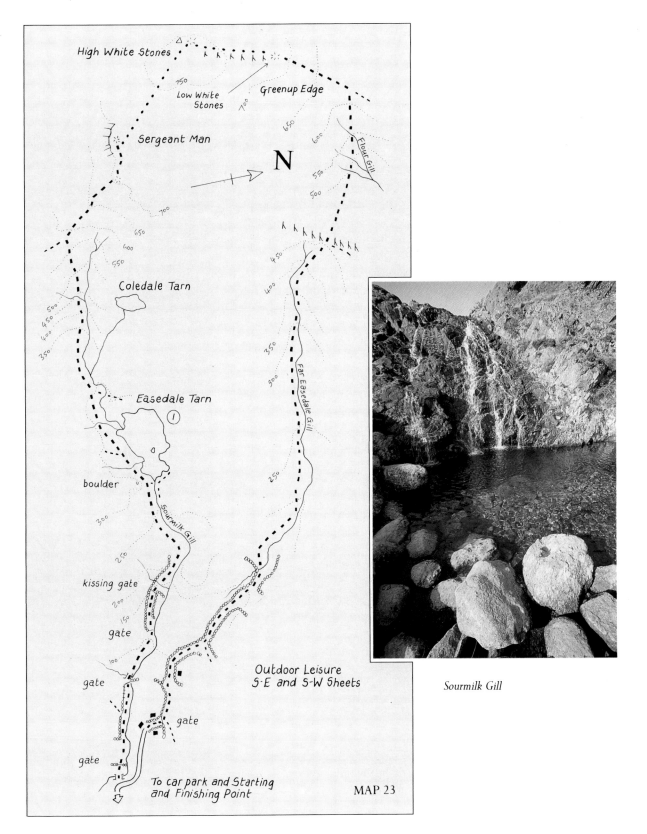

High White Stones

750

Low White
Stones
700

Greenup Edge

Sergeant Man

650

600

Flour Gill

550

500

N

700

650

600

550

450

Coledale Tarn

500
450
400
350

400

350

Easedale Tarn

①

300

boulder

Sourmilk Gill

Far Easedale Gill

250

300

250

kissing gate

200

150

gate

100

gate

gate

Outdoor Leisure
S·E and S·W Sheets

gate

gate

To car park and Starting
and Finishing Point

MAP 23

Sourmilk Gill

into a rough fell field and the footpath starts to go uphill, passing through a kissing gate. The path climbs steadily alongside the beck, past a number of small waterfalls; although no one would include them among Cumbria's most spectacular falls, they are quite impressive—partly because of the way you just seem to happen upon them as you climb the track. The highest of the falls plunges into a small pool—ideal paddling on a hot, summer afternoon.

Continue along the path and it flattens out for a short space before the final pull up to Easedale Tarn (1).

Although there is a footpath which winds round the R of the tarn, it is rather laborious and boggy in places. Instead, keep to the L and walk towards the crag set back from the south-west corner of the tarn. The footpath remains very clear and easy to follow. Ignore a turning L, about half-way along the tarn, which would take you up Blea Crag to Stickle Tarn, and follow the main line of the beck. (Note that on some editions of the OS Outdoor Leisure, South East sheet for this area, the right-of-way deviates from the dotted footpath line and rockets straight up Slapestone Edge.)

The footpath climbs steadily, crossing a series of rock slabs as you ascend. Keep the small beck to your R and eventually you emerge onto a grassy, open fellside. Almost immediately, there is a footpath which crosses the beck to go to Codale Tarn. Shun this, continuing straight ahead until Codale Tarn comes into view on your R.

Keep to the footpath and it takes you up the next set of crags – you need to scramble through a steep little gully at one stage, with the beck running alongside. You come up to a rolling, grassy hillside. The path is well worn in places and is, in any case, waymarked by cairns. Work uphill until the path forks, then turn R. The footpath becomes a little indistinct in places—keep looking for the cairns—but as you slowly climb along the ridge, the distinctive rocky crag of Sergeant Man comes into view ahead and to the L. Hard on your L, there is a good view down to Stickle Tarn and Pavey Ark.

Follow the path round and proceed to the summit of Sergeant Man. This is hardly the highest viewpoint in the Lake District but it is easy to become quite fond of the prospect from here—mainly, I think, because of the glorious view over Stickle Tarn and the Langdales. Turn 90° to your R and you have the massive, central fells of Lakeland, dominated, from this angle, by Great End and Scafell Pike. To the east, the horizon is formed by the long, straight ridge of High Street and below, in the

Easedale Tarn

distance, you can catch a glimpse of Windermere and Rydal Water.

Take your bearings from Sergeant Man by looking north-west across the flat, open plain to High Raise—easily marked by an outcrop of rock topped by a cairn (326° magnetic). Head off towards the cairn, keeping it in view the whole time; the footpath is non-existent at times for the next $\frac{1}{4}$ mile (0.4 km) or so. Just to the west of the cairn is a shelter and an OS obelisk and once again you have excellent views, this time looking north: Skiddaw, Blencathra and, on the far side of the Solway, the remarkable cone-shape of Criffel.

From High Raise, follow a line of old fence posts to head north to Low White Stones, marked by another cairn. Then follow a distinct, muddy path down Greenup Edge and after 600 yards (546 m) the path levels out at a rock outcrop. The path splits here; go R. The footpath is marked by piles of stones, which peter out after a short distance, by which point the path has become more distinct. Cross Flour Gill and bear L, passing a distinctive, jagged rock on your L. The lines of stones resume and lead you across several smaller becks until, after a short climb, you come to the old Cumberland and Westmorland boundary fence.

Today this consists of little more than a line of rusting fence posts stretching between High Raise and Dunmail, with a redundant ladder stile standing squarely on the path in front of you. Cross the ladder stile, for old time's sake (traditionalists will be heard to vilify the 1974 boundary changes) and continue straight down into Far Easedale.

The path meanders down the valley after a steep, rocky start. It is badly eroded in places so it is easy to follow. The beck keeps close at hand, on your right and after 200 yards (182 m) it descends into an unexpectedly dramatic little gorge, overhung by rowan. This is quite delightful and as good as anything on the ascent alongside Sourmilk Gill. Below the gorge, the footpath crosses the beck and continues downhill, past another short waterfall. On a good afternoon this can be a peaceful, relaxing valley, with good views on your L of Helm Crag.

After $1\frac{1}{2}$ miles (2.4 km), the footpath approaches an enclosed field and crosses the beck again via a short footbridge. It broadens out into a track through the bracken and becomes rough underfoot. The beck disappears beneath a stone wall on your R and you continue downhill, following the wall. The path winds beneath oak trees and bear L, around Jackdaw Crag and past three stone-built barns. You come to a junction in the path—left signposted 'Helm Crag', right signed 'Far Easedale'. Continue straight ahead for another, 20 yards (18 m) until you

Looking down on Stickle Tarn from Sergeant Man

arrive at an iron farm gate in the wall on your R. Once through the gate, you are on a broken tarmac track which runs past Easedale House, on your R. Once past the house, turn L onto a metalled lane and walk past a number of small cottages (one bearing the name, 'The Shieling'). Emerging from the group of houses, the lane runs across a meadow to rejoin Easedale Road at Lancrigg House. Follow the road back to the car park.

1 Easedale Tarn

Easedale Tarn was a popular walking route for William and Dorothy Wordsworth, who often used to refer to the valley as 'the black quarter', associating it with the source of all bad weather to hit Grasmere. As you come into view of the tarn, notice the unseemly pile of rubble on your left, beside the path; it is the remains of a refreshment hut which stood here after the war until it was damaged by vandals in the 1960s. A painting of the hut now hangs in the kitchen parlour in Dove Cottage.

Slapestone Edge, incidentally, derives its name from the Scandinavian word *sleipt*, or 'slippery'.

Bow Fell

STARTING AND FINISHING
POINT
Car park at the Old Dungeon Ghyll
Hotel (SW-285062)
LENGTH
$7\frac{1}{2}$ miles (12 km)
ASCENT
2840 ft (860 m)

Another of the popular Langdale ridge walks. After a lung-bursting ascent of Rossett Gill, you arrive at one of the Lake District's two Angle Tarn's (the other lies between Place Fell and High Street). The summit of Bowfell is a rocky scramble, but have your camera ready for a superb view of the Langdale Pikes.

ROUTE DESCRIPTION (Map 24)

Leave the car park via the main entrance to the hotel grounds, as if heading back towards the main road. Just before the bridge over Mickleden Beck, go through the kissing gate in the stone wall on your R (PFS 'Mickleden'). Follow the path between the wire fence and the stone wall, walking alongside a field so that you double back on yourself and pass Middle Fell Farm.

The path winds between the farm and the hotel, beginning a gentle uphill gradient. After 200 yards (182 m), you come to another kissing gate and once through you are faced with a choice of three paths. Turn L (PFS 'Mickleden and Rossett Gill') and follow a rough track, keeping the stone wall on your left.

You are now walking towards the head of Great Langdale valley, with rich pasture away to your L and the more austere features of Bow Fell and Rossett Pike ahead of you. Looking across the fields to Stool End Farm, you can see The Band looming above the farm. The track you are following is easily defined and, although rough underfoot is easy walking. It makes a good approach march to Rossett Gill. As you walk this route, you are directly beneath the Langdale Pikes.

About $\frac{1}{2}$ mile (0.8 km) from the farm, the track goes through a farm gate, with a kissing gate alongside. Once through, the path bears L slightly, still keeping to the stone wall on your L, and you pass through another kissing gate. There is now open fellside on your R on your L the ever-faithful stone wall, which continues for a further $\frac{1}{4}$ mile (0.4 km) before you leave it behind and begin walking across the open valley floor. Now you are ringed by mountains, isolated and challenged by the fells.

Opposite Three Tarns with the Scafell range in the distance

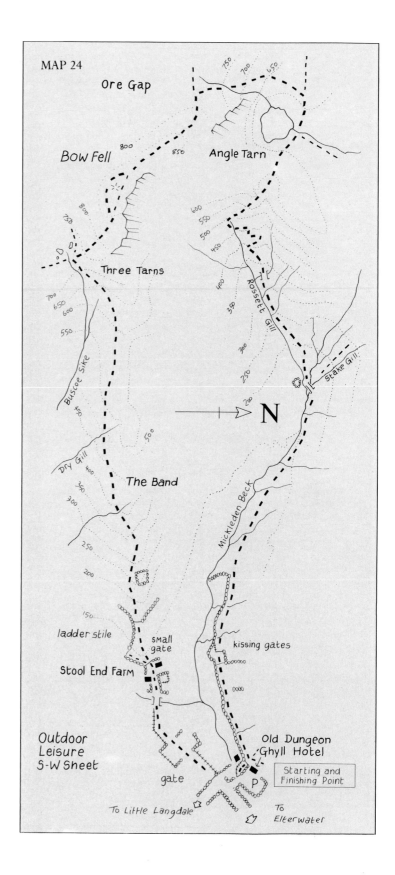

MAP 24

Ore Gap

Bow Fell

Angle Tarn

Three Tarns

Buscoe Sike

Rossett Gill

Stake Gill

N

Dry Gill

The Band

Mickleden Beck

ladder stile

small gate

kissing gates

Stool End Farm

Outdoor Leisure S-W Sheet

Old Dungeon Ghyll Hotel

Starting and Finishing Point

gate

P

To Little Langdale

To Elterwater

Continue marching along the rough track, crossing a beck via a stone-built footbridge and coming alongside Mickleden Beck.

As you approach the head of the valley, the path crosses a wooden footbridge—over Mickleden Beck—and, once beyond a circular sheepfold on your L, splits two ways. Bear half-L (a slate sign in front of you indicates Esk Hause L, Stake Pass R). The path begins to narrow and climb, gently at first, then rapidly becoming steeper, zigzagging alongside Rossett Gill.

The climb is very steep and rough in places, but affords an excellent view over the valley (which is always a good excuse to stop and recover your breath). Finally, after ascending nearly 1000 ft (300 m), the path levels off and you walk over the top to Angle Tarn.

This is a dark, peaceful tarn. Follow the clear path to the R of the tarn. On your L are the grey crags of Esk Pike, whilst to your R is open moorland, climbing steadily towards Glaramara. Keep straight on past the tarn, bypassing a footpath on your right (leading across the moor to Stake Pass). 200 yards (182 m) beyond this path look carefully for another on your L—easy to miss unless you know it is there. At the junction, turn L and begin another steep ascent to Ore Gap.

Towards the top of Ore Gap, the rocks and stones underfoot become very red—evidence of the iron ore hereabouts and a

Bow Fell summit

possible explanation for the derivation of the name. Once at the top, you are on a broad, grassy saddle between Esk Pike, on your R, and Bow Fell on your L. Turn L and begin climbing uphill again across a boulder field. Across the boulders, the path becomes lost but keep a sharp eye out for the odd useful cairn, waymarking the route. Once above the boulders, continue along the rocky ridge to the boulder-strewn summit of Bow Fell.

From this vantage point you get tremendous views back across Lakeland's central fells, dominated by Scafell Pike and Great End. It is sobering to realise how easy it would be, if lost in the mist or benighted, to start off in Langdale and inadvertently come down in Borrowdale or Wasdale (there are few things in life more irritating than descending a fell to discover that you are twenty miles from your car with a mountain in between).

Leave the summit, heading south-east. The slope down to Three Tarns is very steep and rough in places, levelling off just before you arrive at the Tarns (on the descent the path turns to the L at one point to avoid a line of crags).

Three Tarns consists of three or four main tarns and a number of small, subsidiary ponds—their number depending largely upon recent weather conditions. As you approach the tarns, look out for a footpath bearing L, alongside the muddy trickle which flows out of one of the tarns to become Buscoe Sike. As you start to descend, the footpath becomes very clear within a matter of yards and you can see a vivid scar extending ahead of you across The Band.

Follow a broad, gently shelving path, with the beck rapidly dropping away to your R. On both sides are grassy, open fells. This is a long, languorous descent for the first $\frac{3}{4}$ mile (1.2 km), until you begin to come within sight of Stool End Farm. The path drops to a stone enclosure, bearing R to drop away down bracken-covered fellside, arriving at a drystone wall and a farm gate across the route. Cross the wall via a ladder stile. Once on the other side, you will find a seat and a memorial stone in the wall on your L (the slate memorial reads: 'Rest and remember the work of S. H. Hamer, secretary of the National Trust, 1911–1934'). It is a well-sited spot to sit and look down over the valley before beginning the final walk back to the car.

Suitably refreshed, continue the descent to Stool End Farm. As you approach the farm buildings, there are two gates in the stone wall in front of you. Go through the smaller, L-hand gate, around a barn and through the farmyard and onto a metalled lane. Follow the lane across the fields until you arrive back at the main road at the turning for Little Langdale. Continue straight ahead and back to the Old Dungeon Ghyll.

SKIDDAW

STARTING AND FINISHING
POINT
Car park above Underscar
(NW-282254) north of Keswick.
LENGTH
8½ miles (13.6 km)
ASCENT
2180 ft (660 m)

Skiddaw is a friendly, rounded mountain, not too unkind to those who insist on attempting it in plimsoles or wellies. This route, which follows the broad footpath from Underscar car park, must be one of the easiest ways imaginable to ascend a 3000 ft (900 m) peak. The descent requires a little compass work but then it is a straightforward return route, giving you a glimpse of the splendour and isolation of Mungrisedale.

ROUTE DESCRIPTION (Maps 25, 26)

The tiny, windswept car park above Underscar gives a hint of the views you can expect on this walk; already you are high enough to look out over Bassenthwaite and Thornthwaite Forest. Keswick and Derwent Water, however, are largely obscured by Latrigg. Walk to the end of the car park—the opposite end to the approach road—and at the fence cross a stile and turn L (PFS 'Skiddaw, Bassenthwaite'). A muddy path goes between the boundaries of two fields, crossing a stile halfway, and arrives at a farm gate after 300 yards (273 m). Cross the stile alongside and the path forks two ways. The R-hand fork is more of a track. Bear half-L instead and begin to walk uphill. You are now heading back, parallel with the road, having just walked around three sides of the field on your L. The rounded flanks of Skiddaw rise before you.

Memorial to Edward and Joseph Hawell of Lonscale

As you start to go uphill, you will pass a stone memorial cross on your R *(1)*. Keep to the track and the climb gets steadily steeper. The path is a broad, eroded scar at this point, so you will only have difficulty following it if there is snow on the ground. Keep to the fence on your L and, after 800 yards (728 m), you will come to a farm gate. The fence does a dogleg at this point, to cross the path. Climb over the stile next to the gate and continue following the fence, this time on your R. As the gradient eases off slightly, look back and you have wonderful views over Derwent Water and Keswick. Keep ascending, following the fence on your R until you come to a small iron gate. Go through and a very obvious track winds before you,

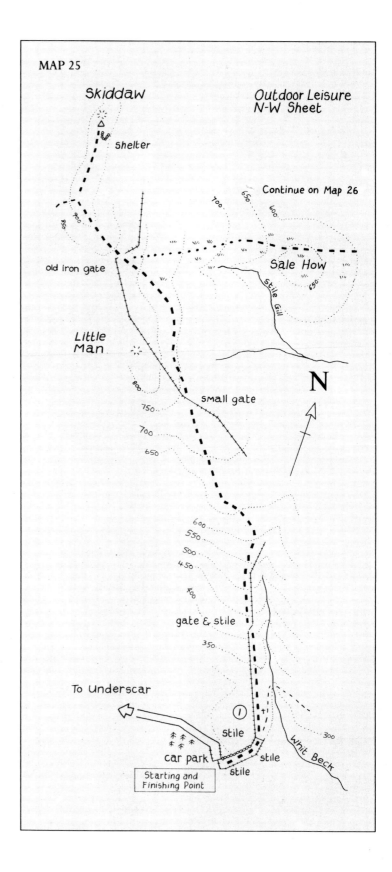

Opposite *Skiddaw from Surprise View*

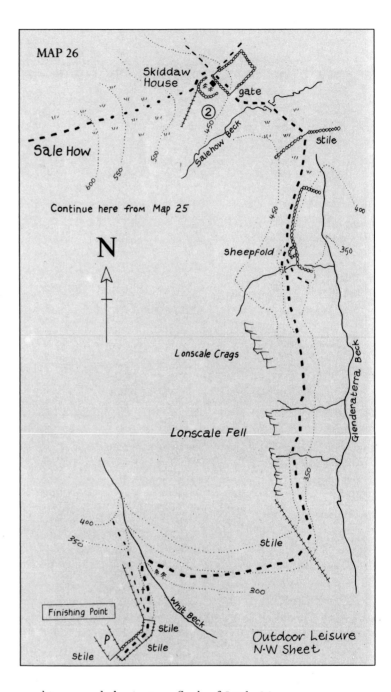

working round the eastern flank of Little Man.

The track remains straightforward and level for perhaps ½ mile (0.8 km) before starting to climb again. You come to a fence—broken in places—and an iron gate. Go through and bear L slightly, making a sharp ascent to the ridge. Follow the ridge to the summit of Skiddaw.

The summit itself is quite crowded; in addition to a stone shelter and an OS obelisk, there is also a stone viewfinder, built in 1977 to commemorate the Queen's Silver Jubilee. Use this finder as a guide to the stupendous 360 degree views.

From the summit, retrace your steps to the iron gate and broken fence. As the path winds away in front of you, stand at the gate and look due east, across a stretch of grassy moorland to Sale How, a small, rounded hill $\frac{3}{4}$ mile (1.2 km) away. There is a distinct track running across the hill, but no apparent footpath between the gate and the start of this track. This, however, is the route to Skiddaw House and our return path. So, leaving the main footpath, head down across the hillside, keeping Sale How directly ahead of you at all times. It remains in view at all times, so there really is no possibility of getting lost.

You hit the start of the track before you reach Sale How. Follow the track over the hill and drop down the other side of Sale How, coming into sight of a wide, river valley and a small, isolated clump of conifers. The track heads directly towards the trees.

One hundred yards (91 m) from the trees, you meet a wire fence and a sheep enclosure on your R. Bear L, along the fence, until you reach the stone wall encircling the trees. Follow the wall L, working round the plantation until you come to Skiddaw House itself *(2)*.

There is a path through the grounds, running in front of the house, but the right-of-way bears L, along the stone wall for a short distance, and then R, to run along the wall in front of the house, keeping the house on your R. Keep to the wall and you walk beyond the house, through a gate and down the track to Salehow Beck. Turn half-L along the beck until you come to a wooden bridge. Cross the bridge and the track meanders across open moorland for 300 yards (273 m) until it arrives at a stone wall. Cross the stile alongside and the footpath bears half-R, away from the wall. Ahead of you is the dramatic, conical shape of Lonscale Fell.

The track starts to climb and runs along an old stone wall on your L. After 400 yards (364 m) you come to a sheepfold, next to the wall on your L, and the path splits two ways. Go half-R and follow the path to a wooden footbridge which spans a tiny, fast-flowing beck. Once over the beck, the path splits again. The path to the R merely cuts a corner, so is only advised if the path below is badly flooded. Go half-L, crossing another beck and continue along the track.

You begin to climb high above Glenderaterra Beck, on your L and find yourself amidst very impressive, rolling fells. The fells of Mungrisedale have an air of wild immensity which comes from sheer size and isolation and has nothing to do with dramatic drops or fierce crags. It is an attractive, little-explored area (but I am not allowed to say more or my walking friends will disown me).

The path levels off below Lonscale Crags. You have now climbed very high above the valley floor and have a good view of the three waterfalls on the opposite fell. Above the line of Blease Fell you can see the cruel ridge of Blencathra.

Continue along the path until you suddenly round the corner of Lonscale fell and Threlkeld and the A66 lies before you (3). Follow the path R, around the grassy flanks of the fell and you come back into sight of Derwent Water.

Almost immediately, you arrive at a wire fence, cutting across in front of you. There are two farm gates and, between them, a wooden stile. Cross and keep following the level grass track. Below you, to the L, you will see an attractive farm, tucked away behind a fold in the hillside. This is Lonscale Farm. Ahead you can see the stone cross and the car park.

Within ½ mile (0.8 km) of the car park, the path suddenly descends into a pretty ravine, with an attractive waterfall. Ford the beck (no proper stepping stones) and bear half-L. Walk uphill, away from this pretty, unexpected spot and the track joins the outgoing path at a farm gate, just below the memorial cross. Retrace your route back to the car park.

1 *Memorial cross*
   This stone cross bears an inscription which reads: 'In loving memory of two Skiddaw shepherds—Edward Hawell of Lonscale, born October 21st, 1815, died June 2nd, 1889, and his son, Joseph Hawell of Lonscale, born December 24th, 1854, died February 20th, 1891. Noted breeders of prize Herdwick sheep.'

2 *Skiddaw House*
   Skiddaw House was built some time during the nineteenth century and was originally the gamekeeper's house, attached to Cockermouth Castle, at a time when Skiddaw forest was extensively used for hunting. It has also, at times, been a shepherd's bothy, and was attached to the Quaker school at Wigton. In June, 1987, it was opened as a Youth Hostel, to provide simple accommodation.

3 *A66*
   One of Lakeland's least attractive features. Built despite fierce opposition from the NPA and the Friends of the Lake District. The then Secretary of State for the Department of the Environment, Geoffrey Rippon, overruled the wishes of the local planning authority and, in 1973, gave the go-ahead for work to proceed. The A66 now roars its way along the western shores of Bassenthwaite Lake to Cockermouth.

View towards Sale How and the return route

3·21

CRINKLE CRAGS

STARTING AND FINISHING
POINT
Car park at the Old Dungeon Ghyll
Hotel (SW-285061).
LENGTH
6½ miles (10.4 km)
ASCENT
2800 ft (850 m)

The delightfully-named Crinkle Crags is the very distinctive ridge which towers above Great Langdale. Some have likened its series of small rocky peaks to the row of knuckles on a clenched fist. This route involves some hard walking in places and includes the 'bad step' above Mickle Door. Any competent rock climber will hardly pause at this 15 ft (4.5 m) high vertical slab, but for anyone less sure of their abilities a good way to cheat is revealed.

ROUTE DESCRIPTION (Map 27)

Walk out of the car park, over the bridge and back onto the main road. Turn R and continue along the road until it forks L for Little Langdale and Blea Tarn. As you stand at the turning, directly in front of you is a farm gate (signposted: 'Stool End Farm'). Go through and follow the tarmac lane across open fields to the farm. (Keep an eye out for a gate bearing a sign which reads: 'If you think you can cross this field in 60 seconds—don't, the bull can do it in 45'.)

Go into the farmyard, past the sheep pens on your R and around a large barn, on your L. To the L of the farmhouse is a wooden gate in a stone wall. Go through and up the stony path in front of you. You come almost immediately to a footpath junction, marked by a slate sign on the ground (L to the Band, R to Mickleden). Go L, ignoring the obvious footpath which you will pass on your R after another 100 yards (91 m). Keep to the stone wall on your L and you are walking along a clear path. Three hundred yards (273 m) from the farm you will encounter another wall which comes down the fell to meet the wall on your L. Cross via the ladder stile and keep straight on, disregarding a track to your L. Eventually you leave the stone wall behind and are following an obvious track, running parallel with Oxendale Beck.

After 200 yards (182 m) you will come to a sheep enclosure. The path bears round to the R of the enclosure (indicated by a small NPA sign) and you find a ladder stile in the wall on your L.

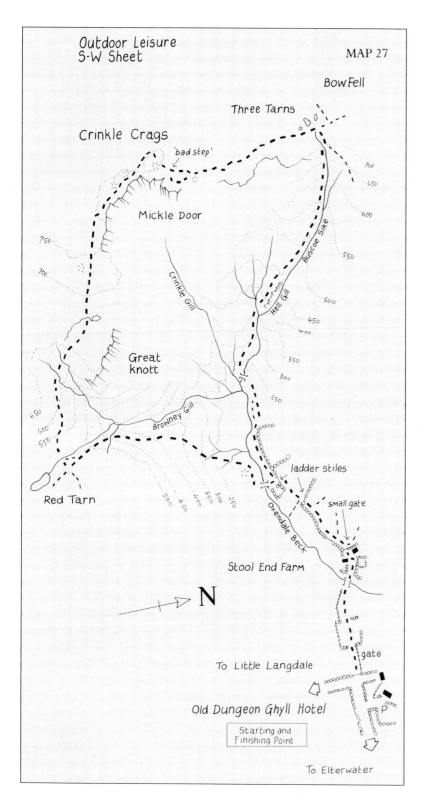

Outdoor Leisure
S-W Sheet

MAP 27

Bow Fell

Three Tarns

Crinkle Crags

'bad step'

Mickle Door

Buscoe Sike

700

650

600

550

500

450

400

350

300

250

Hell Gill

Crinkle Gill

750

700

Great
knott

650

600

550

Browney Gill

Red Tarn

500

450

400

350

250

ladder stiles

small gate

Oxendale Beck

Stool End Farm

N

To Little Langdale

gate

Old Dungeon Ghyll Hotel

P

Starting and
Finishing Point

To Elterwater

Crinkle Crags from Red Tarn

Cross the stile and turn R, following the path until you come to a footbridge.

This footbridge is little more than a giant wooden beam with two narrow handrails; if your rucksack is too large it may be a bit tight to get across. Look out for the two memorial signs on the bridge. Once across Oxendale Beck, the path begins to bear R, marked by cairns. One hundred yards (91 m) from the bridge, at a large cairn the path turns L and you start to climb.

You begin to gain height very quickly. The path is steep and eroded and can be very loose underfoot in some parts. Once above Brown Howe, the path levels off once more and you come into view of a dramatic gorge on your R. Ahead of you is Great Knott, marked by a tremendous cleft in the rocks.

Continue along the path, crossing scree and then beginning to climb again. You have a scramble across a beck feeding Browney Gill, with a small waterfall on your R, and then you arrive at a junction in the path. Bear L, along the flanks of Pike o'Blisco, until you encounter a small cairn. Our route lies R, at this point, but it is worth a quick detour straight ahead to see Red Tarn and a view of Wrynose Pass and Wetherlam.

Having turned R at the cairn, you cross a beck and follow a very clear and eroded path towards Crinkle Crags, quite steep to begin with, then levelling out before a final steep pull to the first of the Crinkles. Scramble onto the rocky ridge of Crinkle Crags and follow the path across the jagged, weatherbeaten rock. There are some wonderful views across to the Langdales and, around from them, right across to Lake Windermere. After following the ridge for a $\frac{1}{4}$ mile (0.4 km), you drop down towards Mickle Door. This is a dramatic cleft on your R, with a good view down to Oxendale. You have now descended to a 'saddle' between the two major ridges of Crinkle Crags and you have a choice of routes before you. Directly in front of you is a loose path which goes up to a 15 ft (4.5 m) slab of rock—the so-called 'bad step'. Although slightly exposed, the climb up this rock is not too bad and, in any case, there is a small gully to the L of the slab and you can work your way up through a gap behind an overhanging boulder. Rock climbers will leap up this route with hardly a thought, but if you have any doubts, there is a path which bears L and takes you round the back of the ridge for 100 yards (91 m) and then climbs back onto the top. Once at the top, bear R, back onto the ridge (the temptation is to go straight ahead, whereupon you will end up on Long Top).

Climb up to a cairn and then follow the ridge again, a long line or rocky summits before you. It is predominantly rough underfoot, with some easy scrambling in places. You get lovely views down into Langdale and Oxendale again.

Eventually, you come to the final descent to Three Tarns. Look for the footpath on your R which takes you down alongside Buscoe Sike and onto The Band. Follow this path for 30 yards (27 m) until you spot a smaller path on your R, on the other side of the beck. Cross over and begin following this path, which, at the start, is marked by a short line of cairns. It is a steep, loose path to begin with, running past a scree on your R. Shortly thereafter, the piles of stones peter out and you are following a route downhill, parallel with the beck on your L.

This is a very rapid descent across a long, grassy slope. The more popular route, down The Band, is much more gradual. It is also more crowded and on this route you soon get a sense of splendid isolation. You pass a very deep, dramatic gorge—Hell Gill. Keep well above the gorge, for once following the OS right-of-way rather than the footpath below. (You get a very good view along the gorge, at one point.)

Once past Hell Gill, the descent suddenly gets very steep and in wet conditions can be treacherous. You descend a rubble scree for perhaps 40 ft (12 m) and come down to a fast-flowing beck. Follow the stream L for 20 yards (18 m), then cross over to a footpath on the opposite bank. Turn L again and follow the path downstream. You descend to a wooden footbridge, crossing just above the confluence of three gills (Buscoe Sike, Crinkle Gill and Browney Gill). Once over, the footpath splits again. Keep to the L-hand fork to give you a view over the beck to the solitary rocky knoll standing above the point at which the three becks meet.

Continue along the path until you meet a stone wall, whereupon the route bears R, without crossing the wall, and then L along the wall at the foot of the enclosure. This easy, level path then takes you back towards Stool End Farm, meeting the outgoing path at the wooden footbridge. Retrace your route back to the Old Dungeon Ghyll Hotel.

Crinkle Crags from Oxendale

3·22

WETHERLAM

STARTING AND FINISHING
POINT
Park at Low Tilberthwaite
(SW-307010), approached from the
Coniston road, just 2 miles (3.2 km)
north of the village.
LENGTH
7 miles (11.2 km)
ASCENT
3075 ft (932 m)

This is not a walk to be undertaken lightly; it is long and it is high. When the weather is bad, review your plans. Wetherlam is on the western rim of the fells and collects cloud. The many slopes, summits and spurs can confuse easily if the visibility is poor. On a fine day, however, the views from this walk are magnificent. It is debatable whether any other single walk gives such an eagle's-eye view of so many valleys and hills.

ROUTE DESCRIPTION (Maps 28)

Turn L out of the car park and follow the road towards a terrace of attractive cottages. Notice the detached National Trust cottage with a fine spinning gallery. Turn L onto a track which takes you past the cottages and through a farm gate. Turn L and follow the path uphill above a steep gorge on your L. After a short distance, the beck makes a distinctive right-angle with its previous course and splits into two. The R-hand arm begins to peter out as the miners' track climbs and starts to take a northerly trend.

You come to a cairn, marking a path to the L. Keep straight on and the path climbs gently to Cove Bottom. The path passes a group of disused buildings and rises above a large, marshy patch (probably caused by natural drainage being altered by two spoil heaps at the mouth of a mine adit, to the R of the track). As you approach another group of disused buildings, a small cairn indicates a path R. Turn R along the new path and climb a short distance to an enormous cairn at a gap in a stone wall. Go through the gap.

You now begin a much stiffer climb, zigzagging up a steep incline onto Birk Fell. When the path finally levels out, you can see down to Greenburn Reservoir and the beck, on your R. The path continues to the foot of a steep, pyramid-shaped ridge, known as Wetherlam Edge. The climb begins with a rock scramble over an inclined slab and at this point things start to get confusing; the cairn-builders seem to have gone slightly mad around here, multiple tracklets winding among the large

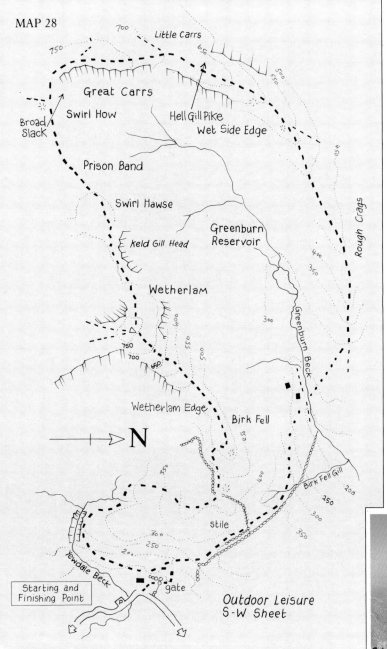

MAP 28

700 — Little Carrs
750
Great Carrs
Swirl How
Broad Slack
Hell Gill Pike
Wet Side Edge
Prison Band
Swirl Hawse
Keld Gill Head
Greenburn Reservoir
Rough Crags
Greenburn Beck
Wetherlam
750
700
650
600
550
500
Wetherlam Edge
300
N
Birk Fell
350
400
Birk Fell Gill
200
250
stile
300
350
Starting and Finishing Point
Yewdale Beck
gate
Outdoor Leisure S-W Sheet

Wetherlam from Swirl How

boulders combine with a plethora of cairns. Continue directly uphill, the scramble approaching a rock climb as you start to crawl on hands as well as feet. Suddenly, you find yourself at the summit cairn, standing amidst a mass of rocky outcrops.

From the cairn, take a compass bearing if necessary; the route to Red Dell Head Moss is not obvious and the line of cairns confidently accompanying the track should be ignored. Swing

away to the R of the cairns, heading in a westerly direction and going downhill.

As you leave Black Sails to your L, the right-of-way traverses the inclined slope above Keld Gill Head before becoming steeper. A small, level, grassy plateau below Swirl Hawse leads to the steep and rocky slope of the grimly-named Prison Band. The ridge is quite narrow at this point. The track ascends to an impressive cairn which marks the summit of Swirl How.

The route on your L leads to the Old Man. Continue straight on, gradually swinging R as the ridge carries you around Broad Slack. The walk along the level, grassy area at the top of the crags is accomplished quite quickly. The next junction is at Great Carrs. Turn R, following the bowl of the hill and descend gently for 2 miles (3.2 km), over Little Carrs, Hell Gill Pike and along Wet Side Edge to the cairn marking an incoming path from the Three Shires Stone. This is a bleak, desolate fell which overlooks Wrynose Pass. A further long descent follows via the grassy ridge above Rough Craggs, to bring you to a point at which you cross Greenburn Beck. There is no bridge or crossing point, but when the beck is high the point just below the little waterfall is well-provided with good footholds.

The crossing point is opposite a group of abandoned mine buildings. Follow the path past the buildings, heading down-stream, until you see a path leading up the slope to your R. If you miss the turning—easily done in this confusing jumble of boulders—carry on until you reach the prominent wall and then turn R, keeping the wall on your L side and walking uphill. Although a right-of-way is marked on the OS map as crossing the lower slopes of Birk Fell, it is not at all obvious.

Once you have crossed Birk Fell Gill, the path becomes easier to follow. It crosses a low stile in a new wire fence. Keep following the wall, ignoring any stiles and turnings on the L. The path crests the rise and heads downhill, close to the wall. A little lower, some pretty cascades follow the little gorge down to Low Tilberthwaite. Turn L, onto the miners' track, and then R at the road, leading to a farm gate. Go through and retrace your steps.

Little Langdale from Wetherlam

3·23

HIGH STREET

STARTING AND FINISHING
POINT
Hartsop village—car park at the end
of the main road through the village
(NE-411130).
LENGTH
9 miles (14 km)
ASCENT
2240 ft (680 m)

High Street, famous as the route of an ancient road which pre-dated the Romans, is probably the most prominent ridge in Lakeland. Visible from most of the major peaks, it casts its shadow far across the plains towards the Pennines. This walk begins by heading away from the more direct routes to High Street, giving you the opportunity to discover Angle Tarn and wonderous views of Martindale. Shortly beyond the summit of High Street, you will encounter one of the tallest—and most mysterious—cairns in the Lake District.

ROUTE DESCRIPTION (Maps 29, 30)

Walk back along the road from the car park, heading towards the village for thirty yards until you see a public footpath sign on your R. Turn R at the sign, onto a rough track past a group of houses until you come to a farm gate. Once through the gate, you are in rough, open pasture land. Follow the stone wall on your L, through another farm gate, heading to a house called 'Grey Rigg'. At the house, the track bears R, in front of the house (PFS 'Patterdale'). After another 20 yards (18 m), you pass through a small gate (notice the house on the rocky outcrop to your right).

A grassy footpath now winds downhill and into the trees. Keep to the main path—disregarding any sheep tracks—and you find you are walking through an attractive mixed woodland, dotted with boulders and bracken. The path meanders gently through the trees for $\frac{1}{4}$ mile (0.4 km) and brings you to a drystone wall, running across in front of you. Cross via a stile and you come immediately to Angle Tarn Beck. Do not cross at this point, but turn L and follow the beck downstream to cross via the wooden footbridge.

From the footbridge, carry straight on along a wide, gravel bridleway. After $\frac{1}{2}$ mile (0.8 km), the track splits two ways; go R, where the route goes uphill and becomes much rougher. You climb quite quickly, to give you good views of Ullswater and Patterdale. The track goes steadily uphill across an open,

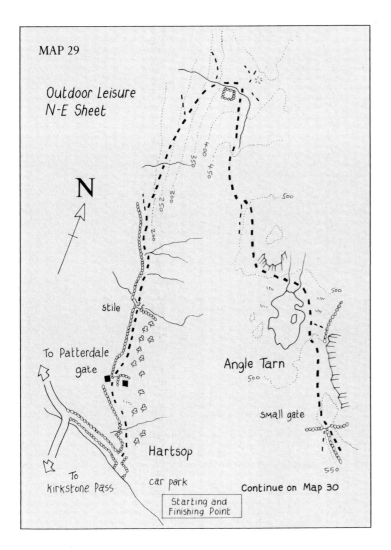

MAP 29

Outdoor Leisure
N-E Sheet

N

stile

To Patterdale
gate

Angle Tarn

Hartsop

To
Kirkstone Pass

car park

small gate

Continue on Map 30

Starting and
Finishing Point

bracken-covered fell. After $\frac{1}{2}$ mile (0.8 km) of climbing, you will pass a path on your L to Crookabeck and Rooking. Carry straight on until you cross Stonebarrow Gill and arrive at a junction of footpaths on a large, grassy plateau. Turn R, past a pile of stones and you have three faint paths in front of you. Bear half-R, back over the beck and heading south-south-east, passing a stone cairn and a sheepfold on your R. You are now on the main footpath to Angle Tarn. All around you is open, undulating moorland, isolated and windswept.

The footpath winds gently uphill and once past Rake Crag, on your L, you get a good aerial view of Goldrill Beck and Brothers Water. Once you have rounded the craggy hump of Angletarn Pikes, there is an obvious fork R, heading off across the fell in the direction of Hartsop. Ignore this and continue past, on the L-hand path, until you suddenly come within sight of Angle Tarn. Less dramatic than its namesake above Rossett Gill, it is somehow more sobre and secretive; it is guarded by a circle of small morains and isolated by a fold in the fellside.

Continue past the tarn, keeping it to your R, and continue along the path, going uphill again and leaving the tarn behind. After 600 yards (546 m), you begin to approach Satura Crag and a stone wall cuts across in front of you. The path splits again at this point. If you go R, following the OS right-of-way, you stay on the Hayeswater side of the ridge. If you go L, however, through a small gate, you make a slight detour, joining up with the main right-of-way at The Knott. This detour is highly recommended for the fantastic view down into Martindale.

Once through the gate, keep to the drystone wall on your R. On your L, Martindale opens up below you. After 200 yards (182 m), the wall becomes a wire fence. Follow it across the fellside until you start to come out onto wild, open moorland, approaching Rest Dodd.

The fence eventually makes a right angle turn, at a point where it meets a drystone wall. Cross the wall and continue along the line of the fence for another 300 yards (273 m); the footpath then bears half-L, away from the fence and towards The Knott. Sulphury Gill creates a muddy scar across the surface of the fellside. Negotiate this as best you can and keep climbing uphill towards the summit, passing through a broken stone wall en route. Just below The Knott, you encounter another stone wall. Turn L and follow the wall around the foot of the hill until you arrive at a junction with another stone wall. Go straight ahead through a gap in the wall, and bear R, around The Knott, passing a blue mountain rescue box on your R.

Just beyond the MR box, rejoin the wall on your R, walking along a superb ridge with High Raise behind you and a dramatic drop to Hayeswater on your R. Follow the path for 600 yards (546 m) until it passes through the wall. Bear L, along the ridge of High Street, with the wall running along roughly the same course, away to your L. Look out for the OS obelisk and cairn, marking the summit of High Street *(1)*.

The wall eventually cuts across in front of you and comes to an abrupt end. Cross through a gap and bear half-R, towards a stone wall and a large cairn, some distance in front of you. The path curves round to the R, across the top of Thornthwaite Crag (ignore a path L, which continues to follow the course of the Roman road down into the Troutbeck valley). Go through the stone wall and you have arrived at Thornthwaite Beacon *(2)*.

From the beacon, head north along the western side of the

Angle Tarn and Angletarn Pikes

wall until you pick up a narrow path, running along the edge of the crag. After 250 yards (227 m), this starts to drop steeply towards Threshthwaite Mouth. You now begin what is possibly the worst descent in the book; the route is marked by cairns as you work your way carefully down 400 ft (120 m) of loose scree. Take your time; the path is well-trodden and stable, for the most part. As you start to reach the bottom, you are on a

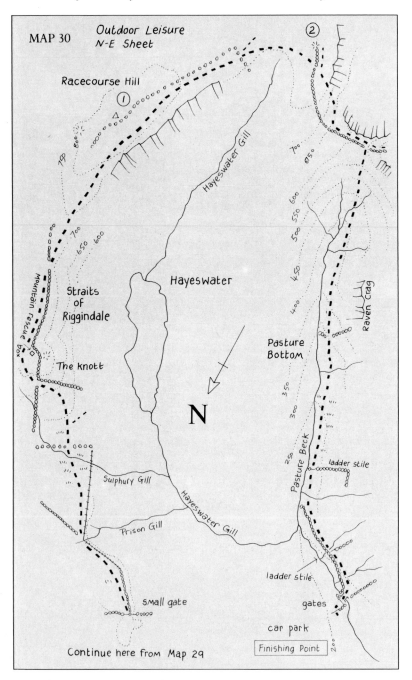

natural watershead between Pasture Bottom and Park Fell Head. To the L you can see Troutbeck Valley and Lake Windermere.

Looking across Deepdale to Fairfield, during an ascent to Angle Tarn

The stone wall from the beacon has descended the crag alongside you and is on your R-hand. Follow the wall until you reach a gap and a junction of paths. Turn R and cross the wall. The path descends steeply in front of you, following the line of a series of reddish, lichen-covered boulders.

The footpath eventually begins to level out as it crosses a large boulder field. Now that you have the opportunity to look about you, you will see that you are in a deep V-shaped valley. A clear path before you winds down to Pasture Beck. Keep to the L bank of the beck, crossing a number of subsidiary becks which feed the main stream.

As you come level with Raven Crag, on your L, the valley floor suddenly drops away and the stream plunges down through a gorge. You realise that you are still high above the valley bottom. Begin another descent, through a boulder field again. 100 yards (91 m) beyond the boulders, a stone wall comes down from the fell on your L and cuts across the path. Pass through a gap in the wall and the path beyond is very easy to follow.

This is a quiet, secluded valley and this route makes a relaxing walk back to the village. About ¾ mile (1.2 km) beyond the wall, you arrive at a well-built wall, topped by a deer fence. Cross via the ladder stile and continue your route downhill until you encounter a third wall. The path bears slightly L and continues with the wall on your R. After a few minutes further walking, you cross another wall and you can see the car park ahead. The footpath runs down to a wide, hump-backed bridge which crosses Pasture Beck. Turn R and cross the bridge, then bear half-L for 10 yards (9 m) and through a farm gate. Follow the wall on your L for another few yards and then a farm gate and kissing gate bring you back into the car park.

1 *High Street*
This long fell ridge is the famous route of a Roman road, which ran from the fort of Brocavum at Brougham, to connect with the main route between Alauna, at Kendal, and Galava, at Ambleside. The road would have taken the easiest path as the fellside and valley would at that time have been rough and boggy.

The summit is known as Racecourse Hill and was a traditional meeting point for shepherds. Each year a fair was held at this spot, with games, wrestling and horse-racing. The last fair was held in 1835.

2 *Thornthwaite Beacon*
This distinctive, 14 ft (4.2 m) high stone cairn can be seen for miles around yet, strangely, its origins are steeped in mystery. In Wainwright's words, it remains 'a fine monument to the skill of its unknown builder'.

Crags by Angle Tarn

HELVELLYN

STARTING AND FINISHING
POINT
NPA car park at Glenridding
(NE-386170), leaving via the entrance
next to the National Park Information
Centre.
LENGTH
8¾ miles (14 km)
ASCENT
2870 ft (875 m)

One of the most popular routes for walkers in the Lake District is the ascent of Helvellyn, via Striding Edge. Except in very icy or wintery conditions, or in high winds, this is a relatively straightforward approach to the summit, along an exhilarating arête. It is not as narrow or as awkward as Sharp Edge on Blencathra. The usual return route is down via Swirral Edge, but this walk modifies the descent to return via Whiteside and Glenridding Common, giving a spectacular view of the two ridges in transit.

ROUTE DESCRIPTION (Map 31)

From Glenridding's new Tourist Information Centre, walk back to the main road and turn R over the road bridge. Turn R again so that you are walking away from the road, on the other side of Glenridding Beck. Continue along the track, past Glenridding Public Hall until you begin to walk along a wooded cart-track. Four hundred yards (364 m) beyond the road you arrive at a Y-junction in the path. Go L, uphill, leaving the river behind.

You come to a picturesque terraced cottage, passing it on the left (it is called 'The Croft'). Once past the house, there is a small gate in the fence on your L with a sign: 'Lanty's Tarn, Grisedale, Helvellyn—either path'. Do not take this diversion but keep straight ahead, through a farm gate. Fifty yards (45 m) past the sign, the track peters out. Cross the little footbridge over the beck on your L and through a gate (PFS 'Grisedale & Helvellyn'). You now follow a footpath which goes steadily uphill, through a small orchard. The path winds to the L of a small plantation of young conifers, following the wire fence on your R and bearing R to a stone wall. Go through the kissing gate in the wall.

Footpath maintenance work may result in diversions on this part of the route; follow the signs where necessary. After walking a few hundred yards across open fellside you come to another stone wall and kissing gate. The path splits just before the gate. Go L—not through the gate—and follow the route

waymarked for Grisedale and Striding Edge. The path meanders over a bracken-covered hillside and drops towards a secluded wood, bounded by a stone wall. Go through a kissing gate into the wood and you find yourself alongside Lanty's Tarn.

Walk past the tarn and the path drops past the dam at the end (ignore a footpath R, just prior to the dam). The path follows the outflow from the tarn for a few yards before bearing R and starting to run parallel with Grisedale Valley. Look—or perhaps I should say 'listen out'—for a farm below, where the local foxhounds are kennelled *(1)*.

The footpath works its way down to a stone wall which comes in from your L, following it until you arrive at a junction of two walls—the second coming down the fellside from your R. Where the path forks, go half-R, walking uphill to pass through the second wall via a kissing gate. Once through the gate, the path splits three ways; you should take the R-hand path, walking uphill.

This part of the route gives an excellent panoramic view over Grisedale. It is a fairly slow ascent, but quite dramatic, with a wide, open fellside rolling away below you. After almost $\frac{1}{2}$ mile (0.8 km) of walking, the ascent becomes steeper and rougher, culminating in a sharp pull up to the stone wall at Hole-in-the-Wall.

The view from this point makes it all worthwhile; you now have a good view of Helvellyn, with Catstye Cam to the R. Look back and beyond High Street you can see the Pennines.

Cross the wall via the stile and head straight once you are over. The footpath levels out to a kinder gradient and you are walking across rough moorland and occasional outcrops of rock. Follow a broad path and after 100 yards (91 m) you come to a good view of Fairfield, on your L.

Follow the line of small cairns and Red Tarn comes into view, lying down to the R in a superb glacial cirque. As you climb up onto High Spying How and Striding Edge lies before you, look on the rock on your L for a small iron plaque; a memorial to one Robert Dixon, killed near here whilst following the Patterdale foxhounds.

There are two routes along Striding Edge—or perhaps one should say, two methods of crossing it. Just below and to the R of the apex of the ridge, there is a path. This keeps just below the top of the ridge and is quite easy to follow. In wet or icy conditions, however, you may find the other method preferable; this is to simply walk across the top of the ridge. Either way, take it carefully and you should have no problem. Although Striding Edge is not as fearsome as its reputation might suggest, it goes without saying that you must be wearing adequate

Opposite Looking west from the start of Striding Edge

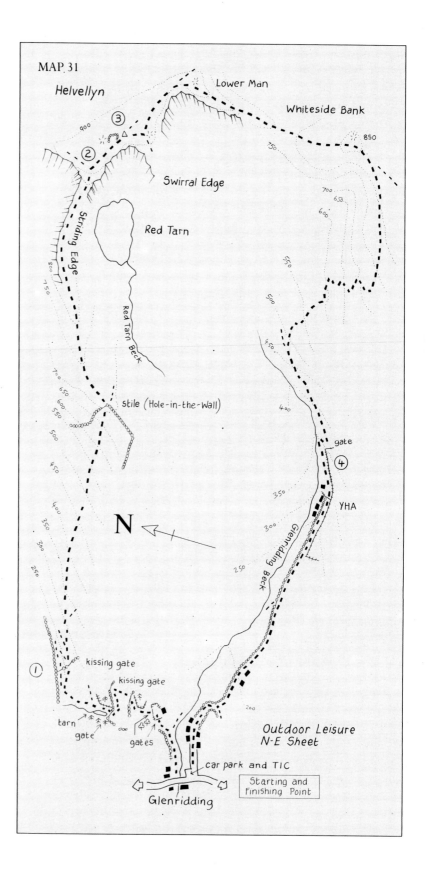

MAP 31

Helvellyn

Lower Man

Whiteside Bank

③

②

Swirral Edge

Striding Edge

Red Tarn

Red Tarn Beck

stile (Hole-in-the-Wall)

gate

④

YHA

Glenridding Beck

N

①

kissing gate

kissing gate

tarn

gate

gates

Outdoor Leisure
N·E Sheet

car park and TIC

Starting and
Finishing Point

Glenridding

footwear. Don't attempt it in wintery conditions unless you know what you are doing. (The only other problem you are likely to encounter is mild exposure from having to stand around whilst queueing up to walk onto the ridge...)

As you come off Striding Edge, there is a short climb down a rock column, known as 'The bad step', then a steep scramble before you arrive at the summit. Bear R, past a memorial stone *(2)* and then half L to a vertical slab—this is the aeroplane stone *(3)*. Continue along the ridge to a stone shelter. A few yards beyond the shelter is the OS obelisk and good views down to Thirlmere.

From the obelisk, head north, following the Red Tarn edge of the summit. After 100 yards (91 m) you will come to a small cairn which marks the descent onto Swirral Edge. Do not follow the path R, but bear L from the cairn and then, after 500 yards (455 m), R at the next fork, to take you down over Lower Man. Follow a broad, rough track downhill for $\frac{1}{2}$ mile (0.8 km) before climbing slightly onto Whiteside Bank. Look back, to the south, and you get a superb view of Striding Edge, with Swirral Edge in the foreground. On a busy afternoon in mid-summer, these two can be so crowded with walkers that they resemble lines with washing hung out to dry. Our route is much more solitary and peaceful—which is what walking the fells should really be all about.

Continue downhill, following the line of stones until you come to a distinct junction in the paths. The stones continue uphill across the broad open fellside of Raise (popular with skiers in winter—there is even a ski tow on the far side). Bear R at the junction and continue a gentle descent towards Ullswater. After $\frac{1}{2}$ mile (0.8 km) the gradient increases and the path follows a series of wide zigzags.

You join a rough track coming down from the old reservoir on your R. Turn L along the track and follow it downhill. As you approach the slag heaps associated with the mines *(4)*, you come to a fence and a farm gate. Bear R, rather than through the gate, and follow the path around the enclosed area. You descend to a group of cottages, now used as an outdoor pursuit centre. Go through the farm gate beside the buildings and, 50 yards (45 m) farther on, you pass a terrace of cottages on your R. These make up Glenridding Youth Hostel.

Follow the track—disregarding any tracks bearing off L to another group of houses—and after 1 mile (1.6 km) you start to come among houses. Follow the lane down to the main road and turn R, back to the car park.

Coming off Striding Edge, with a glimpse of Red Tarn

1 Fox hounds

Fox hunting in the Lake District is a very different sport to that practised in the low-lying southern areas of England. Horses are impractical when following the hounds across open fellside and the only member of the hunt to wear a red jacket is the hunt leader, or 'huntsman'. There are six main packs in Cumbria, of which the Blencathra pack is perhaps the most renowned. The fox hunting season in Lakeland extends from October to late April.

2 The Gough Memorial Stone

This stone tablet, which lies on the summit ridge of Helvellyn, was erected in 1890 by Canon Rawnsley and Miss Frances Power Cobbe. It commemorates Charles Gough, whose remains were found in 1805 at the foot of the crags beneath this spot. The body had been guarded for three months by Gough's dog—a touching example of canine fidelity which moved the poetic muse in both Wordsworth and Walter Scott. Canon Rawnsley was fascinated by the story and went to some lengths to try and identify the excact breed of dog. He published his findings in a slim volume, entitled *The Dog of Helvellyn*.

3 The Aeroplane Stone

Fifty yards (45 m) to the south of the summit shelter stands an unprepossessing stone tablet which bears the following legend:
The first aeroplane to land on a mountain in Great Britain did so on this spot on Dec. 22nd, 1926. Bert Hinkler and John Leeming on an Avro plane landed here and after a short stay flew back to Woodford.

The original, much-eroded stone was replaced in December 1986.

4 Greenside Mines

The mines at Greenside date back some three hundred years and were worked until their closure in 1962. Production was at its height in the early nineteenth century, and it has been estimated that not less than 250,000 tons of lead concentrate has been extracted between the first commercial exploitation in the late seventeenth century and its closure. At one stage, the mine was leased to the Atomic Energy Authority for the purpose of carrying out non-nuclear underground explosions (they were testing seismic instruments, designed to detect underground atomic blasts).

Glenridding Beck was once dammed to provide water power for the mines but, during a storm in 1927, the dams were breached and the village flooded. The flood debris now forms part of the stony peninsula from which the Ullswater launches operate.

3·25

FAIRFIELD

STARTING AND FINISHING
POINT
Car park at Cow Bridge, just north of
Brothers Water on the Kirkstone Pass
road (NE-404133).
LENGTH
10½ miles (17 km)
ASCENT
2515 ft (762 m)

Looking towards Ullswater from St Sunday Crag

Everyone has their favourites but this walk is difficult to surpass. It begins with an easy 'approach march' along the beautiful sylvan valley of Dovedale and returns via St Sunday Crag, the impressive southern wall of Grisedale Valley. St Sunday is one of the best ridge walks in Cumbria—superb on a clear, sunny day when you can look right across High Street to the Pennines.

ROUTE DESCRIPTION (Maps 32–34)

Cross Goldrill Beck by the road bridge, walking into the woods and away from the main road. Immediately on your L there is a farm gate and a kissing gate. Go through and begin walking along a delightful wooded cart-track which leads past Brothers Water *(1)*. This is an extremely pleasant way to begin an ascent of one of the Lake District's most popular summits.

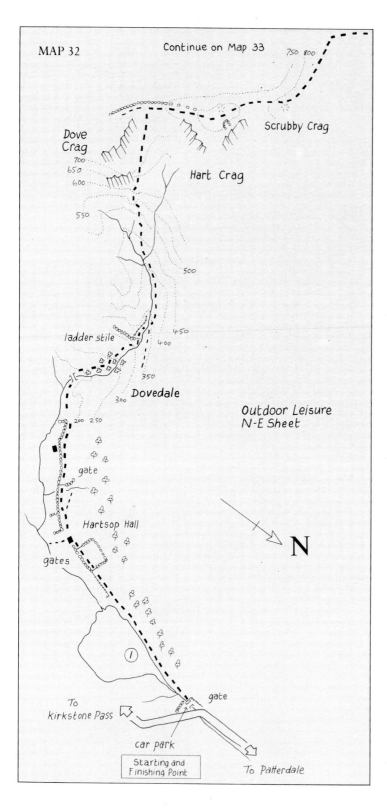

MAP 32

Continue on Map 33

750 800

Dove Crag

700
650
600

Scrubby Crag

Hart Crag

550

500

ladder stile

450
400

350

Dovedale

300

Outdoor Leisure
N-E Sheet

200 250

gate

N

Hartsop Hall

gates

①

To
Kirkstone Pass

gate

car park

Starting and
Finishing Point

To Patterdale

Looking west from Fairfield

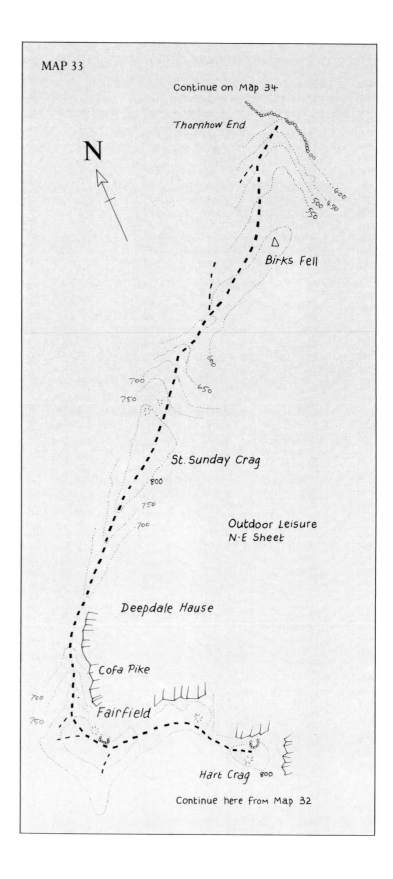

MAP 33

Continue on Map 34

Thornhow End

N

400
500 650
550

Birks Fell

600

700
750
650

St. Sunday Crag

800

750

Outdoor Leisure
N·E Sheet

700

Deepdale Hause

Cofa Pike

700

Fairfield

750

Hart Crag   800

Continue here from Map 32

Just beyond the end of the tarn, the track goes through a wooden farm gate and you start to approach Hartsop Hall, now a farm. Go through another gate and the track bears round behind the farm. Ignore the turning on your L, which leads to Sykeside Farm and campsite, and continue straight on to another group of farm buildings. You come level with sheep-pens on your L and another turning, signed for Kirkstone Pass. Continue past the buildings and, at the next fork, bear slightly L, ignoring the old mining track on your right.

The track crosses a beck and then through another farm gate in a stone wall ahead of you. You are following a wall on your L and pass a large bank barn. As you begin to bear away to the west of High Hartsop Dodd (not as high in 'feet' as Hartsop Dodd, but higher up the valley) you cross a level, fellside field and come to Dovedale Beck. Cross the footbridge which stands just below the line of trees and turn R, to follow the path upstream.

Dovedale is an attractive, wooded valley. The path climbs steadily, passing a number of pretty waterfalls along the way. Once above the trees, you climb to a drystone wall. Cross via the ladder-stile and, 100 yards (91 m) beyond the wall, the path rejoins the back alongside a wire fence. The fence forces you to cross the beck, using the stepping stones. Once over, go straight up the other bank to join a wide track coming in from your R. Turn L along the track and you are heading towards the dramatic cliff of Dove Crag at the head of the valley. The track climbs steeply above the level of the stream and you begin to approach a scree, below the crags. The track becomes a rough path which in turn degenerates into a scramble up a short stretch of scree and rock. Keep to the R-hand side of the scree—marked by a series of small cairns—and you regain a grass path and climb onto open fellside. Continue uphill to the ridge and you encounter a stone wall in front of you, with good views of the Langdales and the Scafell range. Turning round, you can see across the ridge of High Street to the Pennines.

Follow the wall R, away from Dove Crag, keeping to the Hartsop side of the wall. You come to a boulder field and the wall vanishes, to be replaced by a line of small cairns. Follow the path through the boulders. At the top of Hart Crag, the path becomes more obvious. Follow the ridge as it makes a dramatic sweep up to the summit of Fairfield. Looking to your R, you can see the barren, empty valley of Deepdale, contrasting oddly with the lush vegetation in Dovedale.

It is an easy stroll across Rydal Head to the broad summit of Fairfield. The top sports a good stone shelter from which you can admire the views and shelter from the wind.

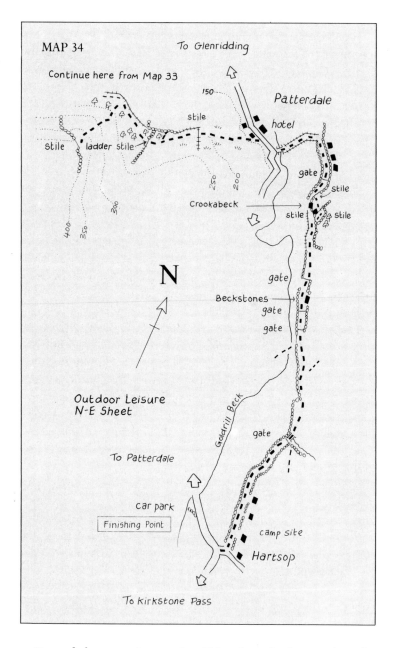

Beyond the summit, you should head north, disregarding the path which bears L and down to Grisedale Tarn. The path drops steeply down Cofa Pike and suddenly you are confronted by the superb ridge of St Sunday Crag.

Walk onto the ridge past a castellated rock on your R and there is a tremendous view of Grisedale Tarn, to your L. You may be lucky enough to cover this part of the route when a low-flying jet passes below you, hugging the contours of Grisedale valley; being able to peer into the cockpits is quite common for ardent fellwalkers. Continue up to the summit.

As you begin to descend the other side of St Sunday Crag, Ullswater opens up before you. The path bears L across the broad, rolling ridge of Birks Fell, keeping to the Grisedale side and you drop steeply over the northern end of the ridge to descend to a stone wall. Look for a section of wooden fence in the wall and cross at the stile. Continue downhill, bearing slightly L, following the cairns.

This part of the walk can be hard on the knees as it drops quite steeply in places and is loose underfoot. Distract yourself by paying attention to the good views opening out in front of you. After another 500 yards (455 m) you arrive at a wire fence. Do not go through the gate but turn R and follow the fence. It joins a stone wall after a short distance and the path begins to bear away slightly but still curving round to the L. Rejoin the wall and keep it on your L until you meet another wall, coming in at right angles from your R. At the junction of the two walls there is a broken farm gate and a ladder stile. Cross the stile and the path bears half-L, across a bog. After 50 yards (45 m), the path splits. Take the R-hand fork over a rock outcrop and the path winds downhill towards another wire fence. Continue over the stile, across a beck and keep R to follow the path to a barn.

Looking east along the ridge towards St Sunday Crag

You join a farm road which bears R around the barn to bring you into Patterdale village, almost opposite the White Lion Hotel.

A suitable pause for refreshments follows. Then cross the road to the pavement and turn R until you come to a small road bridge on your L, crossing Goldrill Beck. Walk over the bridge and continue up the lane towards a group of houses.

You arrive at a T-junction. L goes to Side Farm, so turn R (PBS 'Hartsop'), following the lane past a number of pretty cottages. 150 yards (136 m) beyond the last cottage (Rooking End), you come to a farm gate and once through the lane deteriorates into a rough track. You pass a pair of wooden barns on your L and a hay barn on the R. Just past the barns, look out for a stile in the stone wall on your L. Leave the track here, crossing the stile (PFS 'Hartsop') and following a permissive path across a field for 80 yards (73 m) until you meet up with a stone wall. Turn R along the wall, cross another stile in a section of wooden fence and the path bears round the back of Crookabeck Farm to rejoin the main track. Once on the track, turn L (signed: 'Hartsop') and follow the track.

After a further $\frac{1}{2}$ mile (0.8 km) of the track, three more farm gates and after passing through Beckstones Farm, the track forks two ways. Keep straight on—the R-hand fork leads down to the river at Deepdale Bridge. A little further along the track you pass a footpath on your L which leads to Angle Tarn. Continue along the track until you arrive at Angletarn Beck, which runs across the track in front of a farm gate. Ford the beck and go through the gate. Eventually, after passing a campsite full of log cabins on your L, you come to a metalled lane. Go half-R and follow the lane towards Hartsop village. At the next junction turn R until you reach the main road. Turn R again and follow the road for $\frac{1}{4}$ mile (0.4 km) to arrive back at Cow Bridge.

1 Brothers Water

Most people agree that there are sixteen lakes in the Lake District, but the actual identity of the sixteenth seems to come and go out of fashion. Today it seems to be settled that it is Elterwater, but at one time Brothers Water had the position. Once called Broadwater, the name was changed in the nineteenth century after two brothers were drowned here, whilst skating.

THE OLD MAN OF CONISTON

STARTING AND FINISHING
POINT
Main car park in Coniston village
(SW-304976)
LENGTH
10 miles (16 km)
ASCENT
3320 ft (976 m)

Coniston's 'Old Man' is actually a reference to the mountain's summit cairn; 'man' is the old word for cairn. 2635 feet (803 m) high, this is the southernmost of the major central Lakeland fells. The glorious view from the top takes in both mountains and seascape. The mountain has been so extensively mined in the past and is now so full of holes that it has been described as like 'a maggoty old cheese'. This route, however, avoids most of the unsightly elements and makes an exciting approach to the summit via Buck Pike and the ridge above Dow Crag.

ROUTE DESCRIPTION (Map 35, 36)

Leave the car park via the main entrance and turn L, past St Andrew's Church *(1)* and over Church Bridge. Immediately over the bridge, turn R along a minor road (signed: 'Coniston Station Workshops') beside the Bridge House Cafe. Within 20–30 yards (18–27 m) you have left the village and the traffic behind you and you are walking along a pleasant, tree-lined lane. Continue past the Sun Hotel until you come to a road junction, with an old stone well in the wall opposite. Turn R and follow the road uphill for a short distance. The road bears sharply L (signed: 'Old Man, Walna Scar and Seathwaite'). The road continues uphill. Ignore any side roads and keep straight ahead. You are following a nice, wooded stream on your L and there are glimpses of Coppermines Valley to your R.

As the trees begin to thin out, the road bears L. Ignore the gate (PFS 'Coppermines Valley') in the wall in front of you and keep with the road. Another 10 yards (9 m) farther on, the road turns R again and in front of you is a track to Heathwaite. Stay with the road and the view opens out as you climb uphill. There are fields on either side of you. The old hedge on your L shows distinct signs of the hedgelayer's art.

Three quarters of a mile (1.2 km) from the village, you come

Old Wheelhouse, Coppermines Valley

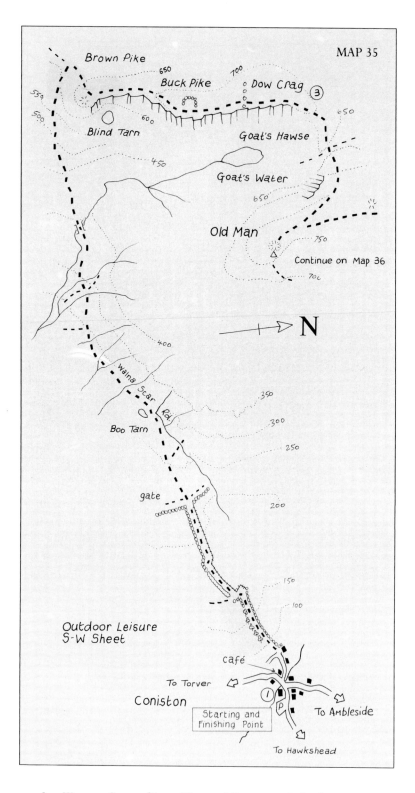

MAP 35

Brown Pike

650

700

Buck Pike

Dow Crag ③

550

600

500

Blind Tarn

Goat's Hawse

650

450

Goat's Water

650

Old Man

750

Continue on Map 36

700

→ N

400

Walna Scar Rd.

350

Boo Tarn

300

250

gate

200

Outdoor Leisure
S-W Sheet

150

100

café

To Torver

Coniston

①

P

To Ambleside

Starting and
Finishing Point

To Hawkshead

Low Water, a glimpse of Levers Water and Coppermines Valley from the summit of Coniston Old Man

to an iron farm gate across the road. Once through, you are on open fellside. Ignoring the track heading R, continue straight ahead. The tarmac peters out and you are on a rough track. Half a mile (0.8 km) on, you will pass another track going R—access road to Bursting Stone Quarry—which you should ignore. Continue past Boo Tarn—little more than a pond on your L, but a good spot for dragonflies.

The track deteriorates as you climb, getting rougher underfoot, though still quite easy to follow. On your L the view has opened out to give a tremendous panorama across to the coast. The 'lighthouse' on the hill above Ulverston is the Hoad Monument. The industrial buildings on the far side of Morecambe Bay form Heversham power station.

One mile (1.6 km) from the gate, the path crosses a beck via a slate footbridge and then splits three ways. Keep straight on and after another 400 yards (274 m) you cross another beck, this time by means of a stone packhorse bridge (somewhat disfigured by iron handrails). From this point there are good views down to Coniston Water; the white house which figures so prominently on the far shore is Brantwood, John Ruskin's home *(2)*.

Once beyond the packhorse bridge, the track begins to zigzag steeply uphill, leaving the flat, open moorland and beginning to climb up into the crags, with impressive views to Blind Tarn screes on your R and, a little further round, the Old Man. This route is known as the Walna Scar Road, an old packhorse route.

You arrive on a flat, moorland ridge. Go R, following an ugly, eroded scar up onto Brown Pike. The views become more impressive the higher you climb.

Continue along the ridge, the footpath being very straight-forward and easy to follow despite encountering slate scree. The going gets rougher as you approach the boulder-strewn summit of Buck Pike, but from the shelter at the top you command wonderful views across the Duddon to the west coast of Cumbria. Below you, to the south, is Blind Tarn and to the north-west, the rounded summit of Old Man.

Ahead of you now is almost 1 mile (1·6 km) of very impressive ridge walking. The footpath, once you climb towards the summit of Dow Crag, becomes indistinct. Keep to the ridge, crossing an old stone wall at one point. As you reach the summit of Dow Crag, Goat's Water comes into view on your R and ahead of you looms Coniston Old Man.

A very rocky descent follows and as you descend, the footpath picks up again. The climb down to Goat's Hawse is overshadowed by the vast, rounded summit of Old Man on your R. At the Hawse, there is a distinct footpath R to Goat's Water and a less distinct one L. Keep straight ahead, following a great,

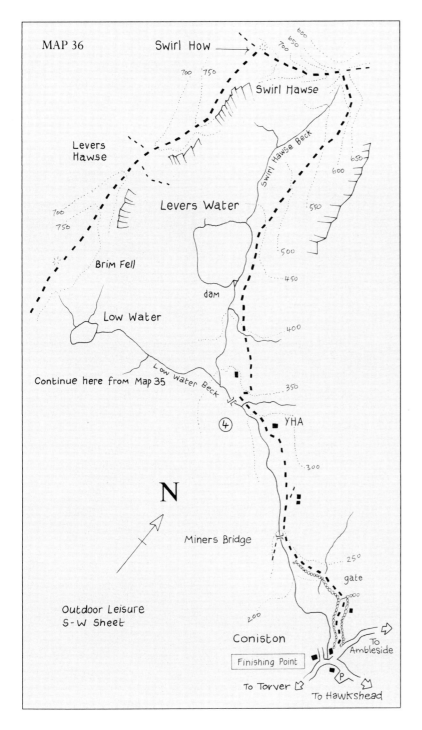

MAP 36

Swirl How

Swirl Hawse

Levers Hawse

Swirl Hawse Beck

Levers Water

Brim Fell

dam

Low Water

Continue here from Map 35

Low Water Beck

④

YHA

N

Miners Bridge

Outdoor Leisure
S-W Sheet

gate

Coniston

To Ambleside

Finishing Point

To Torver

To Hawkshead

eroded scar up the grassy flanks of the Old Man. The path is
very steep to begin with and then, within 300 yards (273 m) of
the summit cairn, it levels off and joins a path coming in from
your L. An easy walk follows along the ridge above Goat Crag to
the cairn.

The view from the cairn—one of the tallest in the Lake District—can be stunning on a clear day, stretching out to the coast, to Ingleborough in the east and to the Furness peninsula to the south. Closer to hand, the large rock face above Goat's Water is Dow Crag *(3)*. (The blue rectangular shape at the foot of the crag is a mountain rescue box.)

From the summit, retrace your steps along the ridge until you reach the path at which you ascended from Goat's Hawse. Bear half-R and follow the path—marked by cairns—along a wide, moorland ridge, to the cairn at the summit of Brim Fell. From here, follow the ridge in a northerly direction towards Levers Hawse. The footpath has become an easy, grassy track with impressive views all round. As you descend past Levers Hawse, there is a striking view of Lever's Water below you.

From Levers Hawse, there is another $\frac{3}{4}$ mile (1.2 km) of superb ridge walking before you climb to the rocky summit of Swirl How. The 8 ft (2.4 m) high summit cairn is most impressive.

From the cairn, bear R down a steep, rough ridge (Prison Band). As you scramble over the rocks, look for signs of quartz beneath your hands. Prison Band extends for perhaps 700 yards (637 m) before depositing you on a grassy 'saddle' between Swirl How and Wetherlam. Turn R and begin the gentle descent to Levers Water.

Although it can be boggy in places, depending upon the time of year, this is a very easy path to follow, keeping the tarn in view the whole time. Situated in a classic, glacial corrie, Levers Water is surrounded by crags on almost all sides—the only opening to the east being the outflow to Coniston and Coppermines Valley. As you reach the rubble-strewn shore of the tarn, work round to the dam and descend L of the beck, below Kennel Crag. As you cross over a small beck, look at the channel—or 'leat'—on your L, once used to take off water to power the mining machinery. Coppermines Valley, a desolate wasteland to some, a rich example of industrial archaeology to others, opens out below you *(4)*.

Five hundred yards (455 m) below Levers Water, the path comes to a snaking L turn and in front of you is a small wooden bridge, crossing Low Water Beck. Ignore the bridge and continue L. The path becomes a disc slate-covered track, passing slagheaps on your L, as you work down towards the Youth Hostel. The track continues past the Youth Hostel, and past a row of converted miners' cottages on your L. Another 500 yards (455 m) farther on from the Youth Hostel, cross a beck coming in from your left via a concrete bridge. Two hundred yards (182 m) beyond that, you arrive at Miners Bridge, which spans the main beck. The rocks hereabout are very pale and the beck falls below Miners Bridge to form a milky-white waterfall. Don't cross the bridge, but continue down the track. The beck on your R descends via a series of waterfalls, foaming rapids and deep pools before cutting through the rock to form a deep ravine thickly overgrown with alder. The track crosses a cattle grid and descends to become a metalled lane. Follow this downhill to emerge in the village at Yewdale Road, beside the Black Bull Inn.

1 St Andrew's Church
St Andrew's Church was built some time during the sixteenth century and is rather a fine building which stands at the centre of the village. The churchyard contains the tomb of Coniston's most famous resident, John Ruskin. There is also a small museum named after him in Yewdale Road. Just as you leave the car park, you should cross to a stone seat on the green opposite; this commemorates Donald Campbell who died on Lake Coniston in 1967 whilst attempting the world speed record in 'Bluebird'.

Church Beck, Coppermines Valley

Low Water from Coniston Old Man

2 *Brantwood*

This was the home of John Ruskin, art-critic, writer, philosopher and champion of many of the social causes of his day. He lived here from 1872 to 1900 and originally purchased the property, site unseen, from one William Linton, for £1500, declaring that 'any place opposite Coniston Old Man must be beautiful'. The house originally consisted of a modest cottage, built by Thomas Woodville around 1797. Ruskin acquired 'a mere shed of rotten timbers and loose stone' but transformed it into a beautiful home which he stocked with books and paintings—including works by Turner, of whom he was an early champion. Ruskin lived the last thirty years of his life at Brantwood and it is now, in accordance with his wishes, open to the public. It must be one of the most beautifully-sited houses in England, with magnificent views across the water to the Old Man.

3 *Dow Crag*

This was once a tremendously popular spot for rock climbers, although in recent years they seem to have favoured the crags of Langdale and Borrowdale. It had an important part to play in the early development of rock climbing as a sport. The first recorded ascent of Dow Crag was made by Walter Haskett Smith and J. W. Robinson, in 1886.

4 *Coppermines Valley*

Digging for copper around Coniston probably dates back as far as the Romans. The first serious impact on the area was made during the sixteenth century by German engineers of the Company of Mines Royal, brought down from Keswick to begin digging for copper. With increasing industrialization, the mines began to dig deeper into the earth and, by the mid-nineteenth century, were reaching depths of over 1000 feet (300 m). They began to decline shortly afterwards as the cost of pumping water from the deep shafts became uneconomic. The mines finally closed at the end of World War I. A railway was built to connect the village with the main line at Broughton and carry ore and slate to the coast.

SCAFELL PIKE

STARTING AND FINISHING POINT
The road approaching Seathwaite Farm, Borrowdale (NW-235122). Do not park or turn round in the farmyard—the farmer will get cross—but there is ample space for parking on the verge of the road. If no luck, use the car park in Seatoller and walk back.
LENGTH
8½ miles (13.5 km)
ASCENT
3160 ft (958 m)

Scafell Pike is 3210 feet (978 m) high, which makes it the highest point in England and an irresistable magnet, drawing even the most indifferent fellwalker to its summit. Its great popularity means that it has one of the highest accident rates of the Lakeland fells; a result of the sheer numbers who climb the mountain, rather than any inherent dangers. Abrupt changes in weather conditions or sudden mist can make it a difficult and confusing peak for the ill-prepared.

There are many routes to the summit, but this is one of the best. It takes in a number of subsidiary peaks and brings you, after a long day's walk, back via the exhilarating spectacle of Taylor Gill Force.

Summit cairn on Scafell Pike—the highest point in England

ROUTE DESCRIPTION (Maps 37, 38)

Walk along the road towards Seathwaite Farm *(1)*, the fells rising steeply on either side of you. To your R is Sourmilk Gill—not to be confused with Sourmilk Gill in Easedale. Walk straight into the farmyard, passing the farmhouse and (in summer) a small cafe on your L. Note well the archway in the barn on your R; you will be returning through here. Continue along a rough farm track and 80 yards (73 m) beyond the farm buildings you will come to a footpath on your L to Borrowdale via Thorneythwaite. Disregarding the path, continue straight ahead, through a farmgate and bearing around to the L of a small group of conifers. You pass through another farm gate as you draw alongside the conifers.

Once past the trees, you are walking across an open valley floor, strewn with rocks and boulders. You can see the path winding up the fellside ahead of you.

You cross a small wooden footbridge and continue along the track to another farm gate. Go through and straight on. So far, you have gained hardly any height. You approach a pretty packhorse bridge *(2)* and cross to the R-hand bank of Grains Gill where you are confronted by a stone wall and yet another farm gate. Once through, there is a junction in the path. Turn L and follow the line of the wall. After 100 yards (91 m), pass through a much-broken stone wall; the track has shrunk to a narrow footpath which is climbing quite steadily above the level of the gill on your L. The path climbs to a narrow gate and goes beyond to bring you to a wooden bridge—White Bridge—which crosses the gill.

There now follows a long stretch of well-maintained footpath (courtesy of the National Trust). Look out for some nice pools in the beck on your R. As you approach the buttress of Great End, the stream plunges through a dramatic gorge. This has a wild, unexplored look and is a good place to look for some unusual species of plant which have escaped the ravages of the sheep. (Whether they also escape the ravages of the gill scramblers is another matter.)

The footpath levels out and to your R is a good view of the reddish scree of Hell Gill, on Great Gable. Carry straight on, towards the towering cliff of Broad Crag and once you have crossed the beck, turn L and follow the stream. As you skirt round the base of Great End, ignore the path to your L and keep to the R. The path climbs and as it levels out once more you arrive at a large stone cairn on Esk Hause. Ahead of you is Esk

Scafell from Scafell Pike

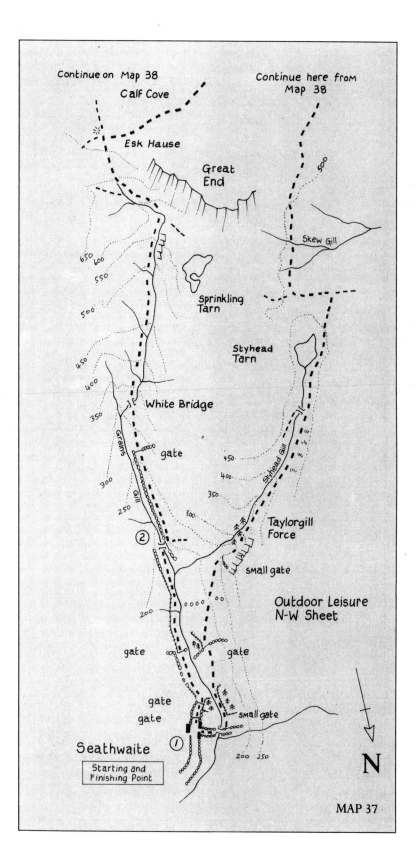

Pike and a good view of the Langdales. Here you find yourself at a junction of several footpaths. Go R, marked by cairns, and continue along a broad scar in the fellside, walking into the boulder-strewn area of Calf Cove.

The track is easy to follow if you keep to an eroded streak across the boulders and levels out once more above the cove. If you walk off the path a short distance at this point, onto a rocky promontory, you have a good view of the head of Wasdale. Back to the path and begin to bear L, up the boulder slopes of Broad Crag. It is $\frac{1}{2}$ mile (0.8 km) of rough level walking to the summit, dropping to a saddle before beginning the final ascent to Scafell Pike.

You follow a sharp, boulder-strewn path up onto the ridge which is once again very rough and steep. Finally, you arrive at the summit cairn (3). You are now at the highest point in England.

From the summit, head north-west, past the OS obelisk, and you can see a path running ahead of you. Keep to the line of

Mountain rescue box at Styhead Tarn

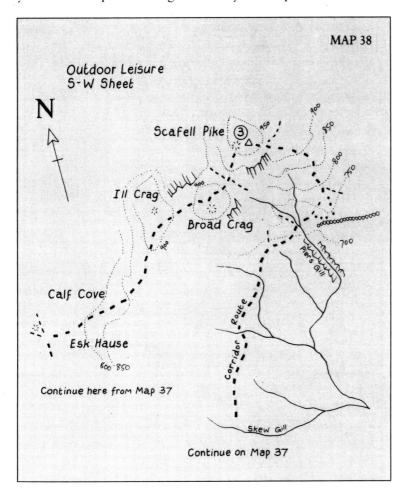

cairns and after 100 yards (91 m), where the footpath divides, bear R. After a steep descent, the gradient eases off and you walk onto a fellside covered in grass—a great relief after the boulders. The path splits again. Go straight down to join a stone wall and a good view of Wasdale, then follow the wall R (without crossing it) until you hit a rocky band coming down from your R and you can then see a path ahead of you which climbs up to rejoin the main track. At the track, bear L and follow it around the base of Broad Crag.

You arrive at Piers Gill, a fierce gorge which plummets down between Lingmell and Great End, towards Wasdale. Cross the head of the gorge and bear L, continuing downhill past a pair of boggy tarns (i.e. do not follow the gorge down). The route leads you to a rock face. Climb alongside the crag (do not go beyond the broken stone wall) and you come up onto the top of Stand Crag, with a view down to Lingmell.

There follows a steep descent to Spout Head and a badly-eroded gully. At a T-junction in the path, go L, following the main track and skirt down to a mountain rescue box. At the box, turn R and walk down to the tarn.

The path follows Styhead Gill downstream and, 500 yards (455 m) below the tarn, you come to a wooden footbridge. The main bridleway crosses the beck at this point but a much more picturesque route is to keep to the L-hand bank and follow the beck downstream to Taylorgill Force. This 90 ft (27 m) cascade is considered by many to be the most spectacular in the Lake District, more for its setting than the actual height of the fall. It stands amidst a small group of conifers and looks out over wild crags to the head of Seathwaite. A short detour to stand beside the head of the cascade is essential.

Walk past the falls onto a narrow path which follows a vertiginous route beneath a steep crag. As you work your way out onto the path you have an increasingly good view of the waterfall. After a very careful 200 yards (182 m), you come to a small gate. Go through, down six stone steps and continue to pick your way downhill.

The path passes through an old stone wall and begins to level out, staying above, but parallel to, the gill. Cross another stone wall via a ladder stile and in the distance you can see a small conifer plantation and Seathwaite Farm. A clear path through bracken lies ahead of you. Continue downhill, past a plantation on your L until you come to the river, passing through a wooden gate to arrive at a footbridge. Cross the river and follow the broad track in front of you, between two stone walls. This brings you back through the archway between the barns. Turn L and retrace your route to the car.

1 Seathwaite

Seathwaite is renowned for having the highest rainfall in England. The actual basis for this is apocryphal, but it does average around 130 in (330 cm) a year. It is not that it rains more often here, just that it rains harder. By comparison, at Keswick, only 8 miles (13 km) away, the rainfall averages only 51 in (130 cm) a year. For the record, Sprinkling Tarn has the highest rainfall; an average of 185 in (470 cm) a year.

2 Stockley Bridge

One consequence of the heavy rainfall in this part of the world is the mass of rocks and boulders which lie across the valley floor, washed down by the beck. In August 1966, there was a tremendous storm and in the heavy flooding that followed, the old packhorse bridge was largely destroyed and had to be rebuilt.

3 Summit Cairn

The summit cairn on Scafell Pike, built in 1921, bears a plaque which commemorates the men of the Lake District who 'fell for God and King, for freedom, peace and right in the Great War 1914–18'.

Grains Gill above Stockley Bridge

The Coledale Horseshoe

STARTING AND FINSHING POINT
A tiny quarry car park, just outside Braithwaite village (NW-227238).
LENGTH
8½ miles (13.6 km)
ASCENT
4200 ft (1280 m)

The Coledale Horseshoe is a stupendous ridge walk, one of the finest in Lakeland. It is also one of the less-frequented routes, which adds considerably to its attraction. A gentle beginning slowly builds up to high level walking over a fine moorland ridge with stunning views at the end. It is hard work and will take you all day, but at the end of it all, the retrospective pleasure is enormous.

ROUTE DESCRIPTION (Maps 39, 40)

Turn R out of the car park and begin walking downhill towards Braithwaite village. Ignore the first footpath on your R (PFS 'Force Crag') and continue to the second (NT sign: 'Coledale'). Turn R and follow the path through brambles to cross a small footbridge. Turn L and walk past a white cottage to rejoin the metalled road at a chapel. Turn R, following the road past Coledale Inn; 600 yards (726 m) beyond the Inn, after passing the last of several cottages, you will meet an iron farm gate. Climb over the stile to the L of the gate and continue along a gravel track to High Coledale, the ruined cottage ahead of you. The track bears R to the cottage; you should continue straight ahead, following a grassy track, working gently uphill. Barrow Gill cuts a deep notch in the hillside on your L and you should ignore the path which swings L to the gill head.

The valley has a broad profile at this point and ahead of you is the triangular mass of Stile End. Five hundred yards (455 m) beyond the cottage, the path starts to bear half-L, passing to the L of Stile End and climbing up towards Barrow Door. At the head of the valley, the path is joined by a little track leading down from Barrow, on your L. Keep going right until the path levels out.

Abruptly the ground to your L falls away to the valley of Stonycroft Gill. As you continue upstream you will spot a

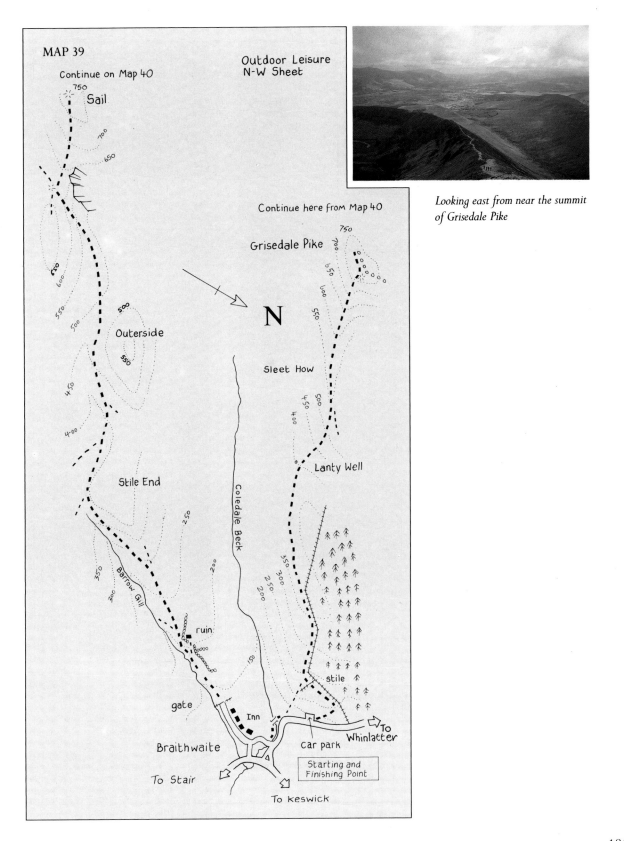

MAP 39

Continue on Map 40

Outdoor Leisure
N-W Sheet

750
Sail

700

650

Continue here from Map 40

650

750
Grisedale Pike

700

600

550

650

600

550

500

N

500

500

Outerside

550

450

Sleet How

400

500

450

400

Lanty Well

Stile End

250

Coledale Beck

350

300

200

200

350

300

stile

150

250

200

350

Barrow Gill

300

ruin

gate

150

Inn

To Whinlatter

Braithwaite

car park

To Stair

Starting and
Finishing Point

To Keswick

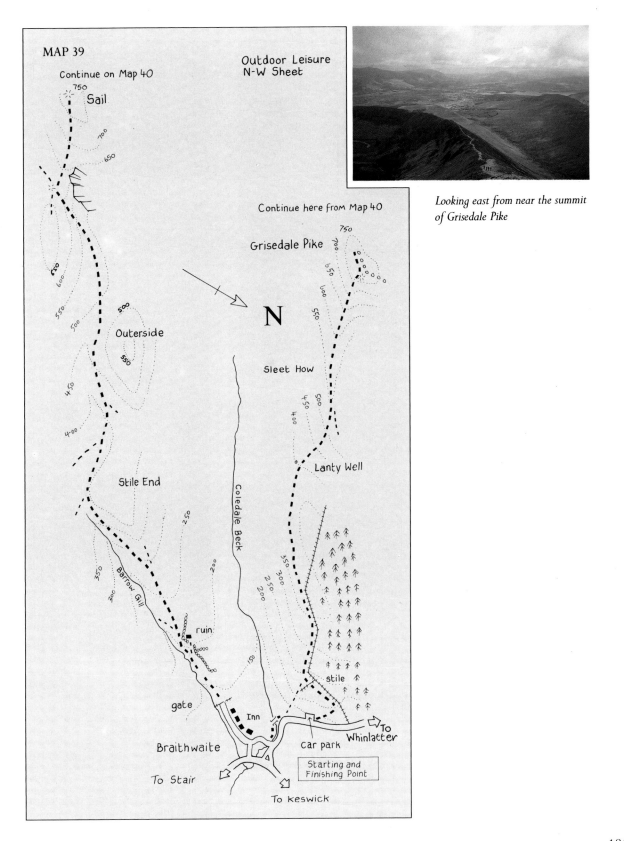

*Looking east from near the summit
of Grisedale Pike*

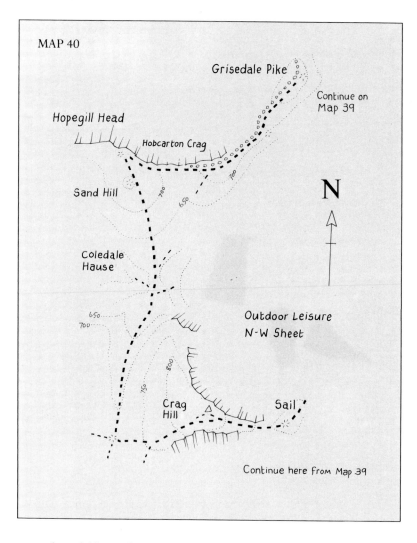

MAP 40

Grisedale Pike

Continue on
Map 39

Hopegill Head

Hobcarton Crag

N

Sand Hill

Coledale
Hause

Outdoor Leisure
N-W Sheet

Crag
Hill

Sail

Continue here from Map 39

sheepfold on the R. Another right-of-way, climbing the valley from Stair, joins your route. At the junction of the two paths, turn R and work your way steadily uphill, enclosed by the bulk of Outerside on your R and the flank of Causey Pike on the far side of the gill.

The path levels out across High Moss, becoming an uncomfortable mess of peat and stones until you regain a flat, grassy area. The hillside drops away ahead of you and, as the path begins to swing slightly L, to run parallel with Coledale Beck, a dramatic view unfolds of Force Crag Mine and the white streaks of High and Low Force.

The path becomes steeper at this point and becomes harder work until you reach the ridge between Causey Pike and Sail. To ascend Sail, take the R-hand track when you come to a

Evening light towards the end of the walk

junction at a small cairn. The track is broad, peaty and eroded and climbs steeply again.

The summit itself is a slight disappointment, despite some good views. Continue straight past the cairn and head slightly downhill to cross a narrow arête, before scrambling up onto the grassy summit of Crag Hill.

Once you arrive at the summit, you will see that the path splits two ways. The R-hand fork leads to the trig point. Go half-L, along a path well-marked with cairns and continue downhill until you arrive at a major junction of paths. Grasmoor lies a little over $\frac{1}{2}$ mile (0.8 km) distant, straight ahead from this point. If you are not visiting Grasmoor, turn R and a broad track leads rapidly downhill, following a little beck. After $\frac{1}{2}$ mile (0.8 km), you will come to a small cairn at a path junction on Coledale Hause.

Coledale Hause is a major intersection, bridging the gap between Eel Crag, to the south, and Sand Hill and Hopegill Head to the north. Go straight across at the junction of footpaths, following a path over Sand Hill to Hopegill Head.

As you approach the point at which the fell ahead of you drops abruptly away, to become the 500-ft (150 m) cliff of Hobcarton Crag, there are impressive all-round views—even across the Solway Firth to the mountains of Scotland. From Hopegill Head, walk in an easterly direction, keeping the cliff to your L and descending to a ruined stone wall. Follow the wall and it eventually brings you, after another $\frac{1}{2}$ mile (0.8 km) to the summit of Grisedale Pike.

At the summit, bear half-R, away from the wall, and begin the dramatic descent to Sleet How. The path is a natural staircase, overhanging the deep valley and the stunning views of Keswick and the Helvellyn range will make you want to take this part of the walk quite slowly.

Once on Sleet How, the stone path changes to fine shale, fringed with heather. Soon afterwards, the heather gives way to bracken as you continue downhill. On your R, across Coledale Beck, is a spectacular view of the earlier part of the horseshoe.

After passing Lanty Well and the edge of the Forestry Commission plantation, on your L, the path becomes a green, grassy track. Wainwright describes this path 'like a lawn' and, amazingly, more than twenty years and many hundreds of fell boots later, the lawn is still intact.

As the track begins to level off, you pass a large boulder. Ignore the track to the R of the boulder and at the wire fence, cross via stile. The gently descending path sweeps round to the R in a huge arc and a set of neat wooden steps deposit you into the car park and the end of the walk.

Opposite A view back showing the final descent from Grisedale Pike

APPENDICES

Access for the Walker

It is important to remember that the designation of a National Park does not alter the ownership of private land within the park boundaries. The laws of access and trespass apply just as much within the Park as outside it.

One of the main objectives of the 1949 National Parks and Access to the Countryside Act was to secure the right to roam at will over uncultivated mountain and moorland. In the event, however, neither the Act nor the designation of a National Park confers this right.

The walker in the Lake District is fortunate in that access has never been a major problem; open fells cover over half the Lake District National Park and walkers have long been tolerated. Free access to the fells is a custom and a tradition.

FOOTPATHS

Despite having the freedom to roam the fells at will, the majority of walkers keep to well-trodden footpaths. The Lake District is covered by a network of over 1500 miles (2414 km) of public paths (including footpaths and bridleways). The origins of this network go back many centuries; the need to connect one farm to another, to connect villages and hamlets, and to connect homes with places of work.

A provision made in the 1949 Act required County Councils in England and Wales to prepare maps showing all the paths over which the public had a right to walk. The final version is known as the 'definitive map' and copies are held at County Council and District Council offices and by some Parish Councils. Public paths can only be diverted or deleted from the definitive map by raising the appropriate Diversion or Extinguishment Order.

PERMISSIVE PATHS

Virtually all the new paths offered by landowners in the Lake District are permissive paths. These can take the form of either entirely new routes or alternatives to existing paths. In the latter instance, a right-of-way through the middle of a crop field may be supplemented by a permissive path which follows the field boundary, with signs encouraging walkers to follow the new route. Permissive paths are often the result of negotiation between the National Park Authority and local landowners. Often, after an experimental period of use, the NPA will apply for a former right-of-way to be diverted to follow the route of the new permissive path.

Ordnance Survey are now beginning to show permissive paths on the metric editions of the 1:25 000 Outdoor Leisure maps.

ACCESS LAND

Under Section 64 of the 1949 Act, the National Park Authority has the power to negotiate access agreements with landowners, whereby the public are allowed access to land held in private hands. In general, however, the Lake District has such an excellent range of footpaths and such a strong tradition of freedom on the fells that such negotiations have in the main been limited to providing lake shore access, new picnic sites and the like. The Stanley Force walk (route 1·1) is an example of access arranged specifically for the benefit of walkers.

Although none of the routes in this book encounter them, properties owned by the Forestry Commission and the North-west Water Authority have in recent years been opened up to the public—for example, Ennerdale Forest and Thirlmere. And, of course, it has long been National Trust policy to allow free access at all times to its open spaces.

All the walks in this book follow either public rights-of-way or alternative acceptable routes.

Finally, it should be borne in mind that due to heavy use footpaths on the more popular fells can become badly eroded and footpath maintenance may become necessary from time to time. If you encounter diversion signs, please follow them rather than sticking rigidly to the routes outlined in the text.

Safety

The golden rules for safety in mountain and moorland areas are:

DO
Carry appropriate clothing and equipment, which should be in a sound condition.
Carry map and compass and be practised in their use.
Leave a note of your intended route with a responsible person (and keep to it!)
Report your return as soon as possible.
Keep warm, but not overwarm, at all times.
Eat nourishing foods and rest at regular intervals.
Avoid becoming exhausted.

Know First Aid and the correct procedure in case of accidents or illness.
Obtain a weather forecast before you start.

DO NOT
Go out on your own unless you are very experienced; three is a good number.
Leave any member of the party behind on a mountain or moor unless help has to be summoned.
Explore old mine workings or caves or climb cliffs (except scrambling ridges).
Attempt routes which are beyond your skill and experience.

Maps

There is a wide range of maps covering the Lake District, some of them good, some indifferent and some apparently wilful. The following, however, are invaluable to the walker:

ORDNANCE SURVEY
Outdoor Leisure maps Four maps covering the Lake District at a scale of 1:25 000 (2½ inches to 1 mile). Now available in metric editions, though

die-hard traditionalists stick to their imperial versions, claiming it's because they like the colours better. All map references in this book have been based on the Outdoor Leisure maps—e.g. SE-408973 refers to the south-east sheet.
Landranger series These maps cover the whole country at a scale of 1:50 000 (approximately 1¼ inches to 1 mile). The Lake District is covered by sheets 89, 90, 96 and 97.

Tourist map The old 1 inch to 1 mile map (scale 1:63 360), though this too is suffering the on-slaught of metrication. Not really suitable for fellwalking, this map is best used for general travel around the area and the occasional low-level walk.

HARVEY MAP SERIES

This is a range of maps aimed at orienteers, but where available they make a useful supplement to the OS maps. Unlike OS, these do not show rights-of-way but concentrate on paths you will actually find on the ground. All are available printed on waterproof paper at a scale of 1:40 000 (approximately 1½ inches to 1 mile), and there are three

available for the Lake District: Borrowdale, Scafell and Helvellyn. The Scafell map is particularly useful as the entire range is on one map, whereas it falls across two Outdoor Leisure maps.

These maps are not available in all climbing and outdoor shops, but can be ordered from:

Harvey Map Series
1 Calderwood Place
Dunblane
Scotland
FK15 9AW
Dunblane (0786) 822494

By the way, the Scafell map is also available as a jigsaw puzzle!

Giving a Grid Reference

Giving a grid reference is an excellent way of 'pin-pointing' a feature, such as a church or mountain summit, on an Ordnance Survey map.

Grid lines, which are used for this purpose, are shown on the 1:25 000 Outdoor Leisure, 1:25 000 Pathfinder and 1:50 000 Landranger maps produced by the Ordnance Survey; these are the maps most commonly used by walkers. Grid lines are the thin blue lines one kilometre apart going vertically and horizontally across the map producing a network of small squares. Each line, whether vertical or horizontal, is given a number from 00 to 99, with the sequence repeating itself every 100 lines. The 00 lines are slightly thicker than the others thus producing large squares each side representing 100 km and made up of 100 small squares. Each of these large squares is identified by two letters. The entire network of lines

covering the British Isles, excluding Ireland, is called the National Grid.

The left-hand diagram of Figure 4 shows a corner of an Ordnance Survey 1:50 000 Land-ranger map which contains a Youth Hostel. Using this map, the method of determining a grid reference is as follows:

Step 1.
Holding the map in the normal upright position, note the number of the 'vertical' grid line to the left of the hostel. This is 72.
Step 2.
Now imagine that the space between this grid line and the adjacent one to the right of the hostel is divided into ten equal divisions (the diagram on the right does this for you). Estimate the number of these 'tenths' that the hostel lies to the right of the left-hand grid line. This is 8. Add this to the number found in Step 1 to make 728.
Step 3.
Note the number of the grid line below the hostel and add it on to the number obtained above. This

FIGURE 4 Giving a grid reference

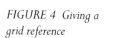
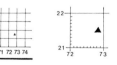

is 21, so that the number becomes 72821.

Step 4.

Repeat Step 2 for the space containing the hostel but now in a vertical direction. The final number to be added is 5, making 728215. This is called a six-figure grid reference. This, coupled with the number or name of the appropriate Landranger or Outdoor Leisure map, will enable the Youth Hostel to be found.

A full grid reference will also include the identification of the appropriate 100 kilometre square of the National Grid; for example, SD 728215. This information is given in the margin of each map.

Countryside Access Charter

YOUR RIGHTS OF WAY ARE

Public footpaths—on foot only. Sometimes way-marked in yellow

Bridleways—on foot, horseback and pedal cycle. Sometimes waymarked in blue

Byways (usually old roads), most 'Roads Used as Public Paths' and, of course, public roads—all traffic

Use maps, signs and waymarks. Ordnance Survey Pathfinder and Landranger maps show most public rights of way

ON RIGHTS OF WAY YOU CAN

Take a pram, pushchair or wheelchair if practicable

Take a dog (on a lead or under close control)

Take a short route round an illegal obstruction or remove it sufficiently to get past

YOU HAVE A RIGHT TO GO FOR RECREATION TO

Public parks and open spaces—on foot

Most commons near older towns and cities—on foot and sometimes on horseback

Private land where the owner has a formal agreement with the local authority

IN ADDITION YOU CAN USE BY ESTABLISHED CUSTOM OR CONSENT BUT ASK FOR ADVICE IF YOU ARE UNSURE

Many areas of open country like moorland, fell and coastal areas, especially those of the National Trust, and some commons

Some woods and forests, especially those owned by the Forestry Commission

Country Parks and picnic sites

Most beaches

Canal towpaths

Some private paths and tracks. Consent sometimes extends to riding horses and pedal cycles

FOR YOUR INFORMATION:

County councils and London boroughs maintain and record rights of way, and register commons

Obstructions, dangerous animals, harassment and misleading signs on rights of way are illegal and you should report them to the county council

Paths across fields can be ploughed, but must normally be reinstated within two weeks

Landowners can require you to leave land to which you have no right of access

Motor vehicles are normally permitted only on roads, byways and some 'Roads Used as Public Paths'

Follow any local bylaws

AND, WHEREVER YOU GO, FOLLOW THE COUNTRY CODE:

Enjoy the countryside and respect its life and work

Guard against all risk of fire

Fasten all gates

Keep your dogs under close control

Keep to the public paths across farmland

Use gates and stiles to cross fences, hedges and walls

Leave livestock, crops and machinery alone

Take your litter home

Help to keep all water clean

Protect wildlife, plants and trees

Take special care on country roads

Make no unnecessary noise

This Charter is for practical guidance in England and Wales only. It was prepared by the Countryside Commission.

Addresses

1 NATIONAL PARK

National Park Officer
Lake District Special Planning Board
Busher Walk
Kendal
Cumbria
LA9 4RH
Kendal 0539 24555

National Park Visitor Centre
Brockhole
Windermere
Cumbria
LA23 1LT
Windermere 096 62 6601

National Park Information Centres (which also operate as Tourist Information Centres) are to be found in the following towns in the Lake District:

Bowness-on-Windermere — Windermere (096 62) 2895
Coniston — Coniston (053 94) 41533
Glenridding — Glenridding (085 32) 414
Grasmere — Grasmere (096 65) 245
Hawkshead — Hawkshead (096 66) 525
Keswick — Keswick (0596) 72803
Pooley Bridge — Pooley Bridge (085 36) 530
Seatoller — Borrowdale (059 684) 294
Waterhead (nr. Ambleside) — Ambleside (053 94) 32729

All are open from Easter to the end of October. In addition, the Centres at Bowness and Keswick remain open until the end of December.

The Lake District National Park Authority also provides a weather service, with up-to-date forecasts for the area and, in winter, fell-top conditions. Available by ringing Windermere (096 62) 5151.

The Park runs a residential centre on the slopes of Blencathra, offering self-catering for groups, families and individuals with excellent field study facilities.
Blencathra Centre
Threlkeld
Nr Keswick
Cumbria
Threlkeld (059 683) 601

2 NATIONAL TRUST

National Trust
Rothay Holme
Rothay Road
Ambleside
Cumbria
LA22 0EJ
Ambleside (053 94) 33883.

The National Trust
36 Queen Anne's Gate
London
SW1H 9AS
01-222 9251

3 MENTIONED IN THE WALKS:

Rydal Mount
Rydal
Ambleside
Cumbria
Ambleside (053 94) 33002

Dove Cottage
Town End
Grasmere
Grasmere (096 65) 544

Ullswater Navigation and Transit Co
    Ltd
13 Maud Street
Kendal
Kendal (0539) 21626 or (for the boat
    pier) Glenridding (085 32) 229

Derwent Water Launch Company
29 Manor Park
Keswick
Keswick (0596) 73013 or (for the
    lakeside) Keswick (0596) 72263

The Ravenglass and Eskdale Railway
Ravenglass
Cumbria
Ravenglass (065 77) 226

Townend House
Troutbeck
Nr Ambleside
Cumbria
Ambleside (0966) 32628

Brantwood
Coniston
Coniston (053 94) 41396

4 OTHER USEFUL ADDRESSES

Cumbria Tourist Board
Ashleigh
Holly Road
Windermere
Windermere (096 62) 4444

Friends of the Lake District
Secretary
Gowan Knott
Kendal Road
Staveley
Kendal
Kendal (0539) 821201

Cumbria Trust for Nature Conservation
The Badger's Paw
Church Street
Ambleside
Ambleside (053 94) 32476

Nature Conservancy Council
Blackwell
Windermere
Windermere (096 62) 5286

Youth Hostels Association (England and
    Wales)
Trevelyan House
8 St Stephens Hill
St Albans
Hertfordshire
AL1 2DY
St Albans (0727) 55215

Youth Hostels Association (Regional
    Office)
Barclay's Bank Chambers
Crescent Road
Windermere
Windermere (096 62) 2301

There are twenty-two Youth Hostels
inside the National Park. The largest is
at Ambleside .

The Camping and Caravanning Club of
    Great Britain and Ireland Ltd.
11 Lower Grosvenor Place
London, SW1W 0EY
01-828 1012

Countryside Commission
John Dower House
Crescent Place
Cheltenham
Gloucestershire, GL50 3RA
Cheltenham (0242) 521381

Council for National Parks
4 Hobart Place
London, SW1W 0HY
01-235 0901

The Long Distance Walkers Association
Membership Secretary
Lodgefield Cottage
High Street
Flimwell
East Sussex, TN5 7PH
Flimwell (058 087) 341

Ramblers' Association
1/5 Wandsworth Road
London, SW8 2LJ
01-582 6878

INDEX

Place names only are included. Page numbers in *italics* refer to illustrations.